Library of
Davidson College

Duquesne Studies
Philosophical Series

EDITORS
Henry J. Koren
and
Andre Schuwer

Titles in Print—Philosophical Series

Volume Six—P. Henry van Laer, The Philosophy of Science.

Volume Seven—Strasser, The Soul in Metaphysical and Empirical Psychology.

Volume Eight—Albert Dondeyne, Contemporary European Thought and Christian Faith.

Volume Eleven—Remy C. Kwant, Encounter.

Volume Twelve—William A. Luijpen, Existential Phenomenology.

Volume Thirteen—Andrew G. van Melsen, Science and Technology.

Volume Seventeen—William A. Luijpen, Phenomenology and Atheism.

Volume Nineteen—Andrew G. van Melsen, Evolution and Philosophy.

Volume Twenty—Remy C. Kwant, From Phenomenology to Metaphysics.

Volume Twenty-One—Joseph J. Kockelmans, Phenomenology and Physical Science.

Volume Twenty-Two—William A. Luijpen, Phenomenology of Natural Law.

Volume Twenty-Three—Andrew G. van Melsen, Physical Science and Ethics.

Volume Twenty-Four—Emmanuel Levinas, Totality and Infinity.

Volume Twenty-Five—Stephan Strasser, The Idea of Dialogal Phenomenology.

Volume Twenty-Six—Andrew G. van Melsen, Science and Responsibility.

Volume Twenty-Seven—Herman H. Berger, Progressive and Conservative Man.

Volume Twenty-Eight—Cornelis A. van Peursen, Phenomenology and Analytical Philosophy.

Volume Twenty-Nine—Martin G. Plattel, Utopian and Critical Thinking.

Volume Thirty—Cornelis A. van Peursen, Phenomenology and Reality.

Sense and Significance

Philosophical Series
Volume Thirty-One

Sense
and
Significance

Don Ihde

Distributed by Humanities Press, New York
for
DUQUESNE UNIVERSITY PRESS, PITTSBURGH

Copyright © 1973 by Duquesne University Press
All Rights Reserved

Library of Congress Cataloging in Publication Data

Idhe, Don, 1934-
    Sense and significance.

    (Duquesne studies. Philosophical series, v. 31)
    Includes bibliographical references.
    1. Phenomenology.   2. Experience.
I. Title.   II. Series.
B829.5.I3   142'.7   72-90635   ISBN 0-391-00313-5

First Printing

PRINTED IN THE UNITED STATES OF AMERICA

FOR my PARENTS

ACKNOWLEDGEMENTS

The essays included in this volume are reprinted with the kind permissions of the following editors and publishing houses:

Chapter 1 first appeared in *Philosophy Today*, Volume 11, Number 4/4, Carthagena Station, Celina, Ohio, editor, Robert Lechner.

Chapters 2, 3, and 5 originally appeared as "Studies in the Phenomenology of Sound" *International Philosophical Quarterly*, Vol. X, No. 2, June 1970, editor, Norris Clarke S.J.

Chapters 4 and 8 were originally published in *Phenomenology in Perspective*, edited by F. Joseph Smith, and in *Facets of Eros*, edited by Erling Eng and F. Joseph Smith, reprinted by permission of Martinus Nijhoff, Publishers.

Chapter 6 first appeared in the *Journal of the British Society for Phenomenology*, Vol. 1, No. 3, October 1970, editor, Wolfe Mays.

Chapters 7 and 10 appeared respectively in *The Southern Journal of Philosophy*, IV, No. 2, 49-54, copyright © 1966 by the Department of Philosophy, Memphis State University, and in VIII, No. 4, 399-408, copyright © 1970 by the Department of Philosophy, Memphis State University, reprinted by permission of the editor, William B. Barton, Jr.

Chapter 9, published in the *Journal of Thought*, January 1967, editor James J. Van Patten.

Chapter 11 appeared in Vol. XXVII, No. 4 of *Philosophy and Phenomenological Research*.

Chapter 12 appears originally in this volume, but is scheduled to appear in *Phenomenology and the History of Philosophy*, edited by J.R.A. Mayer.

Chapter 13 reprinted by permission of Quadrangle Books from *New Essays in Phenomenology*, edited by James M. Edie, copyright © 1969 by Quadrangle Books, Inc.

Chapter 14 appeared in *Horizons of the Flesh: Critical Essays on Merleau-Ponty*, edited by Garth Gillan by permission of the Southern Illinois University Press.

Special acknowledgment goes to Thomas F. Slaughter, co-author of chapter 6, professor Slaughter previously a graduate student at Southern Illinois University when this chapter was written, is now a member of the Afro-American Studies Program at Rutgers University. The author also wishes to acknowledge the assistance provided by Southern Illinois University and the Research Foundation of the State University of New York for the financial assistance provided by summer research fellowships which made the writing of these essays possible. Finally, acknowledgment is due professor Andre Schuwer of Duquesne University and Mr. John Dowds of Duquesne University Press for their helpful encouragement and assistance in the preparation of this volume.

CONTENTS

Introduction 13

PART ONE. PERCEPTION

A. THE EXPERIENCE OF SOUND

CHAPTER   1. *Some Auditory Phenomena* 23
               2. *On Perceiving Persons* 35
               3. *God and Sound* 42
               4. *Auditory Imagination* 47
               5. *Listening* 61
               6. *Parmendian Meditations* 69

B. THE EXPERIENCE OF SIGHT

               7. *Parmendian Puzzles* 82

C. THE EXPERIENCE OF TOUCH

               8. *Sense and Sensuality* 91

PART TWO. LANGUAGE

               9. *Rationality and Myth* 107
              10. *Language and Two Phenomenologies* 117

11. Some Parallels between Analysis and Phenomenology 131
12. Wittgenstein's "Phenomenological Reduction" 142
13. Language and Experience 155
14. Singing the World 162

Index 183

INTRODUCTION

Philosophy is both an experience of the world and a thinking about that experience of the world. The Greeks claimed that the love of wisdom began in wonder. Oriental sages claimed that it began in suffering. But both rooted philosophy in experience—without this source philosophy soon withers and dies. In this respect philosophy is like the relationship between certain wysteria vines and the trees which they use as their hosts. The vine reaches the height it attains by encircling and climbing the trunk of the host tree, eventually reaching above the height of the tree itself. But, once in a while, the vine kills the very tree which supports it thus dooming the vine to a fall or death itself. Only so long as the tree continues to live can the vine stand full in the sun.

Phenomenology as philosophy begins in a call to return to the richness of human experience as the base for all subsequent knowledge. Of course phenomenology is not the first philosophy to issue this call. In our own American traditions in philosophy the "Golden Age" of pragmatism in the thought of John Dewey, William James and George Herbert Mead there was once such a call. But phenomenology is the more recent arrival and has the audacity to claim a rigor and comprehensiveness not often matched in philosophic investigation. Phenomenology begins its climb towards the sun by looking at the full ranges and possibilities of human experience.

In this phenomenology is timely. There is a pregnant readiness for the recollection of primal experience, particularly among students of recent years. Dissatisfied with the past, upset by the implications of the future, bored by the desert landscapes painted by the dominant forms of philosophy today, youthful thought has once again taken the turn towards the birthplace of philosophy. The battlecry is experimentation—"to the things themselves" even at the risk of sometimes desparate results. The search for alternate lifestyles, the flirtation with non-western forms of thought, even dangerous and often damning drug experience are all symptomatic of this experimental attitude towards experience.

I do not wish here to advocate phenomenology as a quick or simple therapy or salvation scheme in this arena where Western Civilization may be fighting a dying battle. But I do hold that only in a milieu open to experimentation can phenomenology begin to make its way. One cannot appreciate, much less understand, phenomenology without a sense of experimentation. The tribal language of "perspective variations," "free fantasy," "intuiting essences," concerns a careful and imaginatively directed concern with the limits and possibilities of experience.

In its Husserlian beginnings phenomenology was thought of as a new "science of experience" beginning in descriptive psychology. If the science metaphor is understood in its best sense as an open ended, exploratory, exciting in discovery interrogation which results in *not* leaving things as they were, then it is indeed appropriate. Perhaps phenomenology is like science in another sense as well. To perform as a creative theoretical thinker it is necessary to change perspectives. The scientific thinker must abandon or at least suspend certain long held and habitual beliefs about things. He must begin to think in a new and often radically different way.

I remember the initial shock afforded me as a college freshman when taking my first serious course in the physical sciences. The professor, in order to justify his distance measurements between the earth and the sun, constantly regarded "nearly parallel" lines as parallel. I was appalled that science would begin by "cheating." My literal turn of mind was keeping me from entering the theoretical attitude which allowed the professor to "see" what he saw.

Eventually I learned from these "lies." Once their pedagogical usefullness began to open new vistas of thought which in turn allowed one entrance to undreamed of territory, the excitment involved in the theoretical attitude became irresistable. Phenomenology, like science in this respect, is also a conversion in perspective. Those who wish to learn phenomenology merely by reading texts, even those of the masters of the art, will remain essentially blind until this perspective is gained.

Those philosophers who constantly accuse phenomenologists of being "unclear," besides subtly attempting to make all the world fit into their mold, are often confused precisely because they have failed to discern the radical conversion needed to "see" what is to be seen. Their literal-mindedness is no different in kind than that of the perennial "common man" who historically fails to inhabit the imaginative perspective which allows the new to be seen. The "common man" of the Copernican era, insofar as his positivistic holding to his earthbound perspective holds, was quite correct in insisting that the sun sets and rises. But he also fails to see the possibility of inhabiting a different perspective, the imaginative perspective which places the thinker at that point which allows one to "see" that the earth moves around the sun. The Copernican abandons that earthbound context to inhabit this previously forbidden standpoint. Moreover, what the Copernican says must remain a hopeless confusion to the listener until the listener can "see" from the point of view of the new standpoint.

Phenomenology's conversion is similar in type and calls for the inhabiting of its own perspective—only it wishes to attain a universal end in placing the whole realm of experience and its possibilities under scrutiny. Why is it and how is it that we inhabit perspectives? And, how is it that within these perspectives there are characteristic "shapes" to our views such that there is always an area taken for granted? And how do we take that which is taken for granted and make it the theme for discovering precisely what constitutes the perspective which we often did not even know we had previously inhabited? Phenomenology's conversion is such that its first aim is to make all which has been familiar strange.

To say that phenomenology is a different perspective is not yet to show what is seen from that perspective. Showing is what I am attempting in these essays. They begin simply with common areas of experience, with the "familiar" experiences of hearing, seeing, and touching. They are first a kind of descriptive psychology which is the first step towards the more radical implications of phenomenology. I begin with the simple question: what *does* "show itself" when I experience sound, sight, and touch?

I have tried to avoid too much tribal language. In their original forms these essays were addressed to different audiences at different times. They do not even demand that one be a phenomenologist to understand—but they are invitations to begin to look at the world phenomenologically. My philosophical "technology" is, as it were, submerged. I do presuppose the "phenomenological reduction" and only when that is ultimately seen can these essays be understood to be more than descriptive psychology. Husserl held that the psychology which becomes possible within phenomenology is ultimately justified and grounded only transcendentally, after the psychology can be viewed as transcendental itself. It was here that the radicality of the change of perspective is seen for what it was implicitly all along. The phenomenologist may begin with the "lie" that descriptive psychology is a starting place—but his aim is a transcendental turn towards an ontology of human experience.

But even the beginning calls for a few methological notes. The "phenomenological reduction" which provides the basis for the perspective may be simplified in this context as a set of investigative "rules." (1) *Suspend explanations, describe.* This rule is simple to state, but in fact difficult to effect. Phenomenology calls for the suspension of "theories" which attempt to go behind or under experience, for a suspension of "constructs" which are elaborated to account for such and such a phenomenon. In this phenomenology seems at first to be both anti-scientific and anti-metaphysical. In actuality its aim is to be *pre*scientific and *pre*metaphysical. Thus all physiology, all psychological theories which would account for experience on the basis of something unexperienced are "bracketed," placed out of play.

Does this mean, then, that the phenomenologist seeks some "pure" experience prior to theorizing? Is there a "pure" description? The answer must be *no*. The rule is a directive aim—it has a particular function in getting phenomenology started. It is a way of directing one's "looking." The descriptive rule turns out, in practice, to have two sides. First, it directs one's attention to what appears within whatever context is being questioned. It is a call to center one's focus upon the "thing itself."

It is almost amazing how much we, the actual experiencers, take little note of our experiences. The descriptive rule asks that we pause and look carefully at what we experience. It usually does not take long, once so directed, for us to begin to note many things that either we were unaware of or only vaguely aware of before having our focus so directed. Nor is it long before the serious investigator of experience begins to be overwhelmed by the sheer complexity of this richness. A frequent first result of attempting to describe is to encounter a certain sense of limitation in being able to describe the phenomenon. Words seem to fail one and one finds himself struggling with language, with metaphor, with new ways to express what is discovered. In this respect the early result of description is counter-traditional, counter-conventional. But it is this because of what the "things" teach us.

There is also a complementary function to the descriptive rule. The purposeful suspension of our habitual explanations also begins to create an awareness of how powerful and constant these taken for granted predispositions are. We begin to find our "world" is clothed with ideas as Husserl contended. Our expectations and beliefs not only guide *what* we see, but coupled to the first function of the descriptive rule, begin to be understood not only as a habitual guide but also as a way of "overing over" much of what is possible within experience.

The descriptive rule in both its functions is the phenomenologist's version of the scientist's "lie" which pedagogically shocks us out of our initial literalmindedness and opens to us a new way of viewing things.

(2) *Vary possibilities.* Once the descriptive way is opened the first foray into the field is expansive rather than reductionist. Already the curious investigator may suspect that our previously vague or unnoted experiences hide more wealth than expected and that if one such simple conversion shows the way to this that other discoveries lie ahead. This suspicion is what lies within the phenomenologist's use of perspective and imaginative variations.

One seeks to exhaust, insofar as possible, the full range of possibilities lying within any given region of investigation. Again the rule is simple to state but difficult to practice. How can one exhaust possibilities? But also again the question belies a misunderstanding of the role of perspective variations. The function of variations is to further open the field of investigation and to preclude too rapid closure. Its aim is to problematize experience in such a way that most of the usual theories of experience are forever seen to be oversimple reductions *of* experience.

Within this technique of variations I often have students utilize what I call a catalogue of experiential aspects. For example, within a given duration of time note as many features of what goes on as possible. One usually finds (a) that an amazing multiplicity of phenomena occur and (b) that in taking note of this multiplicity one's awareness gradually becomes more and more keen in relation to what is "observed."

(3) *Seek structures.* The use of variations does not stand alone. If its function is to prevent reductionism and to expand the field and complexity of the field to an almost endless set of investigations, it needs a complementary rule. Phenomenology seeks not only the richness of

experience, but its "shape." It seeks the structures of perception, of language, of the lifeworld. Variations are supposed to gradually reveal those structures both in terms of their boundaries and in terms of their characteristic features. Through variations the famed "resistance of the invariant" is to be found—although not all invariants are clear and distinct as Husserl so well discovered. There are "inexact essences" just as there are "concepts with blurred edges."

The catalogue device, fortunately, is not the only means available to the phenomenologist. Often there is an all-at-once experiential availability to a structure. For example, in many of my essays I refer to the encompassing character of the Sound field, sound "surrounds" one. Cataloguing may detect this but only very clumsily, but in the paradigm case of listening to music this quality of sound experience becomes immediately available.

One word of caution is due here. A serious problem confronted by phenomenologists is the temptation at too fast closure. It is all too possible to discern features that in their context and dimension are clear enough, but upon further investigation turn out to be related to a wider context and deeper levels of phenomena so that what is initially taken as "apodictic" turns out to be relatively "inadequate." In relation to the investigations reported here if the attention to the experience of sound has taught me anything it is that no sensory realm is so limited or so clear in structure that *direct* implications can be drawn from it. In fact some of the apparent "anti-visualism" expressed in my earlier essays on sound I now perceive to be unfair to vision—the problem today is not the reduction of a world to a seen or visualist world, but a reduction *of* vision itself. But I did not appreciate this without the lessons learned in the investigation of auditory experience. Perception lies imbedded within a tradition of interpretation and the first lessons of the descriptive rule must be returned to again and again.

Perception is seen here to have another side, inextricably bound to our sensory experience of the world in our "linguistic" experience of the world. Ultimately phenomenology cannot speak of perception *and* of language, its "unit" of meaning is perception-language, or better said, being-in-the-world. Thus the second part of the collection though differing in style belongs to the same question embodied in the nascent whole of these essays. How is the philosopher to understand his being-in-the-world?

The reader should probably not approach this collection with the expectation that the latent whole is what is important. Rather, the parts should excercise their own separate interests. This is really an *introduction* to phenomenology. Each essay should therefore stand alone as well as in relation to the others. This is particularly apparent with the several essays on sound. There is often a minor repetition at the beginnings of these articles because they appeared in various magazines, but each takes its own direction and emphasis. In the second section some of the essays were directed to specific problems, but again the directions are multiple rather than single. Reading, like the beginning of phenomenology, should let the things teach what they will. If there is a unity to the question which animates these essays it will show itself.

Phenomenology is both an experience of the world and a questioning of that experience. But the philosopher's experience of the world is also a transformation of the meaning of the world. In that lies the excitement of philosophical investigation.

PART I.
PERCEPTION

CHAPTER ONE

Some Auditory Phenomena

The task of this paper is to point up certain phenomena which I believe have been neglected in philosophical investigation, i.e., *auditory phenomena*. In their most explicit relation to the history of philosophic discussion auditory phenomena would probably be considered within the larger problematic of the relation of perception to understanding or of sense and reason. It is my implicit contention that it may be wise to undertake a more complete examination of the phenomena of auditory perception—and of imagination—prior to arguing general implications for epistemological theory.

I should indicate from the very beginning that my investigations take place within a general philosophic commitment to phenomenological procedures. I hold to that tradition which contends that prior to tracing implications and relations one must examine the phenomena of experience. What I say about auditory phenomena is guided by the idea of phenomenological reporting at this point largely within the limits of what Husserl would have called *phenomenological psychology*. I should also indicate that when I use the terms "perception" and "imagination" I refer to descriptions of immediate experience and not to theories about perception and imagination which attempt to account for or to explain our experiences.

My explicit strategy is to begin with observations upon what I claim to be a narrowness in the traditions of philosophical discussion of both perception and imagination. (a) I first indicate that the mainstream of philosophic discussion of perception and imagination has often centered in visual models, metaphors, and understandings of the world. (b) Secondly, I seek to display what I take to be frequently ignored or hidden aspects of perception and imagination in terms of auditory phenomena. In this case I employ a descriptive and suggestive contrast between visual and auditory modes of perception. (c) Finally, by uncovering certain unique characteristics of auditory phenomena, I move to a brief description of auditory imagination which leads to the uncovery of a dual primacy of language and perception.

Thesis 1: *In questions of both perception and imagination philosophical discussion has largely resorted to visual models and metaphors.*

Early in our philosophic tradition Aristotle announces that:

> Above all, we value sight; disregarding its practical uses, we prefer it, I believe, to every other sense, even when we have no material end in view. Why? Because sight is the principal source of knowledge and reveals many differences between one object and another.[1]

One might even return to philosophy prior to Aristotle and find a similar affirmation concerning visual perception. Heraclitus claims, "Eyes are more accurate witnesses than ears."[2] In both cases it is the accuracy for distinctions which stands out. I suspect that even the later tradition of "clear and distinct ideas" in Cartesianism is also a visual metaphor. When one adds the notions of "insight," "intuition," "models," not to mention the many common expressions for understanding such as, "I see what you mean," the great emphasis upon the visual in both literal and metaphorical senses begins to emerge.

The importance of visual metaphor for thought in even its most abstract and theoretical uses is sometimes noticeable. One could almost endlessly suggest possibilities from the history of philosophy. For example: when Berkeley claims that we do not have any general ideas present to the mind because only specific ideas are so present, does he mean that we cannot imagine in a visual sense anything other than a specific triangle or a series of successive triangles? Or, when certain commentators upon current scientific theory remark that we have replaced picturable models with sheer mathematical ones does this mean we have finally moved out of the range of visual modelling and metaphor? Finally, note

---

1. Aristotle, *Metaphysics*, translated by John Warrington (London: J. M. Dent and Sons, Ltd., 1956), p. 51.
2. Wheelwright (ed.), *The Presocratics* (New York: The Odyssey Press, Inc., 1966), p. 70.

the great importance of visualizable graphs, such as the existential graphs of Peirce, for the teaching and understanding of logic.

The emphasis upon the visual is not less absent in phenomenology and existentialism. Indeed, one might well say that with Husserl's consistent use of *Anschauung, Wesenschau, Sicht, Eidos,* etc., the emphasis upon "seeing" and visual metaphor becomes more and not less pronounced. Sartre, in his discussion of other persons, again places the problem in terms of "the look."

To this point I have merely isolated a few examples which illustrate some ways in which visual models and metaphors have been frequently used in philosophical discussion—just as the same point could be made for visual metaphor on common speech. But if philosophy does rely upon such a visual emphasis the result is not inconsequential. A preoccupation with the visual has, in my opinion, at least two more important consequences: (a) In the first place the constant emphasis upon the visual in both perceptual and imaginative areas has the effect that a similarly extended investigation into auditory phenomena is frequently ignored. The reasons for this may be several, but I suspect that philosophers may often accept an "aristotelean" visual tradition as the most obvious place to discuss sense and perhaps go on to assume that whatever problems emerge there would apply equally well in the domains of the other senses. (b) But ignoring a certain area of phenomena may also have the effect of *hiding* what may be important and unique data for further consideration. It may be that hidden or ignored phenomena such as those of the audible may hold implications for a more general understanding of philosophical modelling processes.

We might begin by asking: Do all senses have the same characteristics? In what way is each sense unique? And what implications does each area of sense have for philosophical thought? For not all perception nor all imagination is visual in character. We are creatures of auditory perception and auditory imagination as well. Here we might do well to listen to the advice of Empedocles as well as to see the wisdom of Aristotle:

> Come now, with all your powers discern how each thing manifests itself, *trusting no more to sight than to hearing*, and no more to the echoing ear than to the tongue's taste: rejecting none of the body's parts that might be a means to knowledge, but attending to each particular manifestation. [italics mine][3]

---
3. *Ibid.*, p. 127.

For while it is not necessarily the case that Aristotle and Heraclitus were wrong about the distinction and accuracy of the visual witness—in relation to the appearances of enduring objects—it might be that an examination of auditory phenomena would yield quite different insights.

Recently I found a sympathetic ear in the person of F. Joseph Smith of Emory, who incidentally is trained in both music and philosophy. Smith independently arrived at some of the same notions I had developed in a paper on Perceiving Persons.[4] In his paper, "Insights Leading to a Phenomenology of Sound," he notes:

> And yet it is necessary to do more than look into the situation. And perhaps it is precisely here that our great teachers fail us, in that they still make use of visual metaphor and the language of sight. In seeking the full phenomenological spectrum we may have to do more than just look into things . . . (he goes on to question Aristotle's assertion and adds) musicians of that time, whose ear was attuned to far more subtle tonal nuances than ours, and who had no such reliance on written music as we do . . . would not have been able to agree with Aristotle. . . . For most musicians feel that the sense of hearing is far more perceptive and profound than that of sight, since sound reaches to the very center of our being.[5]

Smith goes so far as to call for an examination of *akoumena* rather than the visually suggestive *phenomena* of the dominant tradition.

Thesis 2: *While there are certain common structural characteristics to every mode of perception each sense has its own distinctive mode of being.*

To get at the distinct characteristics of auditory phenomena as over against visual phenomena one needs a technique of reduction to purified phenomena. It is here that phenomenological reporting and reduction are important. The aim is to successively explore the region of auditory phenomena paying strict attention to the presentation of the phenomena.

Unfortunately this is not so simple as it might seem an ordinary introspection or casual noticing will not do. (a) In the first place the objects within our experience and our experiencing of them is global. We

---

4. This paper was presented at the Society for Phenomenology and Existential Philosophy, October 20, 1966.
5. F. Joseph Smith, "Heidegger and Insights Leading to a Phenomenology of Sound" (unpublished paper), pp. 2-3.

find ourselves thinking, seeing, hearing, being in a certain mood, having a certain bodily feeling, and so on. This is in no way to say that our experience is a buzzing, blooming confusion, because it isn't. It takes no apparent effort to experience in this globally primary way at all. One might add that it is our analysis which characterizes experience as multi-dimensioned. (b) But we can also focus or concentrate upon a given dimension of our experience. And here the problem is to focus upon the way in which auditory phenomena present themselves. (c) But even this is not completely sufficient because our listening, both perceptually and imaginatively, is imbedded in habits and beliefs and theoretical considerations which may further confuse the issue. Our language, for example, displays visual imagery in relation to auditory phenomena quite frequently: "That was a brilliant sound." "A very bright little piece of music." "Oh, what a clear voice." These habitual and theoretical considerations hinder our getting at a reduced or purified auditory world. Phenomenologists have as a first rule the "bracketing" of such consideration in order that concentration upon the phenomena may be more complete.

Now while I presuppose a phenomenological reduction as a technique one can "short-cut" the method for purposes here if one is willing to resort to suggestive and often metaphorical language to point up the phenomena we wish to isolate. The ultimate appeal in the process is to a careful examination of your own experience. Finally, I employ one other "short-cut" by supplying a guiding clue as a heuristic device.

My suggestion is this: visual phenomena *tend* to be *spatially oriented:* auditory phenomena *tend* to be *temporally oriented*. This clue is probable open to a number of modifications if we pursue the matter to its ultimate extreme—but if we follow this clue at first certain notions emerge.

To play up the contrast let us first concentrate upon the "spatiality" of sound—how does sound present itself to us? Case #1: We are in a room in which a stereo set is playing a Beethoven symphony; the sound is turned up enough to cover all background sounds. In this case if one were to ask about the "spatiality" of sound he might be tempted to describe it as either too poor or too rich. If we were asked to locate sound as we might locate a material object then phenomenal sound is too poor in a spatial sense. To be sure, we might be able to locate a certain general direction as the origin of the sound—especially if we use our eyes as a guide (we see the speakers). But if we reduce our experience to consideration of pure sound then the direction of sound becomes less precise (hide the speakers or blindfold the listener. Note, too, the interesting phenomena of seeing a person talk in an auditorium and hearing him "as if" the sound were coming from his mouth despite the fact that the speakers are located at the sides of the room). Even here we might be said to be able in a very general sense to locate the direction of sound due to sound clues such as relative loudness near the speakers, etc. But in spite of all this the precise location of sound is too poor to count as a basis for identifying particular spatial position.

Thus we might turn to the other temptation and say that sound is too rich in its spatiality. We might say that sound surrounds us; we are absorbed in the music; sound is fullness; or, for my own preference, sound is in "parmenidean fashion" a complete and well rounded whole. In either case, spatial poverty or spatial wealth, the spatiality of sound is not the same as that of sight.

With visual phenomena the case is normally otherwise. We are able to locate objects within a field with describable precision. The chair is on the right of the table; the blackboard is behind the desk; the book is on top of the shelf—and if these descriptions are not accurate enough you may add measurements down to millimeters.

Finally, if one attempts to apply visual spatial relations in a strict sense to auditory phenomena the contrast becomes sharp: It would be odd to say, in listening to the Beethoven symphony, that the sound of the oboe is to the right of the bass viol or that the sound of the trombone was in front of the sound of the cornet.

This does not mean that sound lacks its own distinctions and precision. For there are other dimensions to auditory phenomena. The symphony is presented as a totality—but within that totality further variations can occur. Case #2: In a given passage the strong section plays *forté* but the other instruments "recede" to *pianissimo*. That is, within the totality of sound certain sounds "stand out." Note that even in this description the metaphors of visual space may well intrude themselves— yet strictly speaking we ought to say the sound of the strings is stronger, auditorily more penetrating, than that of the other instruments. The relations are not spatial ones at base at all.

We might be able, with effort, to elicit a language which does not revert to visual and spatial imagery if we wish to make more precise the mode of sound presence. The "standing out against the background" of sound against sound is auditory and not visual or spatial. One might better say that there is a "sounding out above sound." But we must admit that our words are ordinarily too poor to entice exactly the sense of sound presence.

Case #3: Another dimension of auditory phenomena similar to the piercing presentation of one sound in relation to the other is the ability we have to select from a field of sound certain given sounds. Again, as the symphony presents itself as a totality, I can within limits select out certain instruments. I can focus my auditory attention upon the flute rather than upon the violin or, for that matter, upon the symphony as a whole. I can make this sound "stand out" against the background— within limits. That is, within the sound world I can isolate dimensions of sounds almost as if they were individuals.

But here I must be careful, for my speech opens itself to a spatializing and thus visualizing of sounds. I have broken up Sound into sounds; I have made the totality a series of parts. But is it necessary that this occur? I suspect that one reason sound appears "poor" is that we demand that it be of the same structure as visual phenomena.

Now I grant that the use of visual metaphor is so strong that even blind persons talk about "seeing" though it should be noted that their seeing is a hearing and a feeling. Their learning to use the terms correctly cannot have been from visual experience.

Since, for the present, we seem doomed to visual metaphor, I should like to suggest that rather than a model of discrete spatial individuals for the auditory world, we ought to employ a fluid-dynamic model. Sound, if we speak of spatiality at all, is like a fluid which surrounds us but it is a fluid which contains dimensions of varying shades and viscosities—nor is this imaginative model out of keeping if physics holds any truth. We claim, after all, that that gaseous totality, air, carries sound to us.

The global encompassing of sound is a pervasive sounding which seems, as Smith remarks, to penetrate to the center of our being. My control of sound is less complete and less spontaneous than my reaction and control of vision. A flash of bright light can make me blink my eyes; I have but to easily shut them if I wish to close off the obvious world; or I can turn my head to avoid seeing a painful spectacle. None of these escapes or controls is so easy with sound. When the children are fighting in the next room they can "get to me" in a hurry for I cannot avoid them except by removing my presence; by placing my fingers in my ears;

or by insulating and soundproofing my study. Turning my head may help me to hear a barely audible sound—but it will not shut off a loud one. Sound pervades my world and it invades my being.

Thus I would note that sound is "spatially poor" in respect to discrete individuals; but it is "spatially rich" in its fluid ability to flood and intrude itself upon my consciousness—perhaps it is this one characteristic which turns the metaphorical table upon sight when we talk about "loud colors." But let us now turn the coin around and examine temporality, following our clue that sight is temporally poor when compared to auditory phenomena.

In the history of philosophic thought enduring, stable, and usually fixed objects have frequently provided a norm for discussion. Much ink has been used to discuss doors, tables, and chairs (or when we think about unchanging substances) they seem to be permanent fixtures of the world. This is the case whether or not something "underlies" them. Such statics of metaphysical discussion often never rise to the question of temporality.

Yet the puzzles of time are among the most difficult and complex for philosophical investigation. I suggest that part of this difficulty may well lie at the door of the quasi-visual norms we have allowed to dominate philosophical literature.

Even within the visual domain one can find an approximation to the difficulty of time. While most discussion seems to be directed to enduring and seemingly almost timeless or changeless entities, the more difficult discussion has been had over how to deal with motion. For even within the visual domain motion entices a sense of time. Time is inseparable from motion whereas stable objects may be said to allow time to "float over them."

But now turn to auditory phenomena. The ever-changing presence of sound is time-ful. Sound is in normal situation never static. Its coming into being and its passing from being is continual in its variation. The world of sound is one of fury save in ideal situations or in exceptional isolation in a desert. I suspect it is not without reason that Husserl turns to musical experience when he describes the protentive and retentive characteristics of internal time consciousness.

The constant temporality of sound presence is almost total, and, despite those who would maintain that nature is mute, the presentation of varied sound occurs there as well. At my summer home in the mountains of Vermont the world is surrounded with sound. It may appear to be quiet—by contrast to the Honda culture of Carbondale—

but it is not silent. From bubbling stream to babbling bird to breathful wind the mountains are full of sound.

By contrast the two situations which would be the most shattering and eerie would probably be complete silence or the presence of a single, unending note of sound. In either case the timeful variance of sound would suddenly become de-timed and one might well be disoriented. In the rare cases when there is an absence of sound many persons comment that time becomes unreal or stands still.

Now to this point concerning time and sound I would like to add a higher level speculation which I find extremely enticing but have yet to fully work out. Scholars have long remarked that one of the distinctive elements in our cultural past was the development of a philosophy, or better a theology of history among the Hebrews. A sense of history and historical consciousness was acutely present with this Semitic tribe in comparison to their surrounding neighbors. Note that among other aspects of their cultural outlook was a unique theology of the Word. Word, for the Old Testament thinkers, was not a stable structure in the later Greek sense of *Logos*, but was rather the expression of a "willful" power through breath.

Word, for the Hebrews, was living or timeful word. In addition, the Hebrews held an absolute prohibition against *images* or representations of God. God could not be visually represented. Visual representation was idolatry and the prophets mocked idols because of their static lifelessness. But curiously enough, there were no prohibitions against God manifesting himself in Word. Indeed, it was through Word that God did manifest Himself. Could it be that the strong sense of temporality and history has its basis in a theology of the word in more than a metaphorical sense?

Again, independently, F. J. Smith has made a similar point:

> Speech is a thing of sound, not a phenomenon, but an akoumenon ... Nothing I am saying is appearing to you in the full sense of what I aim to be at this time. My words, as alive, as "acoustical phenomena" are what bring meaning ... (Just as in) prophetism the sense of hearing is foremost, for the prophet must listen to the God and then in turn must speak for the God to the people. It is the dialectic of listening and speaking that is at the basis of a phenomenology of prophetism.[6]

---

6. *Ibid.*, p. 3.

This last speculation, however, opens still another area for investigation of auditory phenomena. Certainly spoken and heard language is to be found within the larger spectrum of acoustical phenomena. Here I turn to a more specific examination of the experience of the audible in relation to language.

Thesis 3: *The auditory presence of language is an almost total constant of experience.*

This statement may at first seem odd. Yet I think it can be supported by an examination of our on-going experience. In the first place allow me to underline what should have been obvious, but which is frequently unnoticed, i.e., that all the language of vision, the metaphorical and imagistic language, may be *said* and not *seen*. The auditory phenomena of my speaking may be the basis for visual imagery. Spoken and heard language is the enticer of visual imagery and not the other way around. While visual models may be basic for our understanding ultimately I would argue that language is more basic and that language is first thought, spoken and listened to within the domain of auditory phenomena.

Now when I claim that the auditory presence of language is an almost total constant of experience, I do not nor could I maintain that one constantly hears audible speech in a perceptual mode. Thank goodness for the fact that outside universities people are not constantly talking! I perceive language only when it is spoken or when I say something out loud myself.

However, I do, so long as I am conscious, "think." And here I have immediately entered deep water—but allow me to foolishly tread this angelic domain of fancy. My sub-thesis is that a very explicit form of thinking is an *inner speech* which I would like to call an *auditory imagination*. Now I am open to a rather vast series of misunderstandings which might occur because "thinking" as we employ it covers so many types of conscious activity. I would not wish to deny that the phenomena of thinking are much more varied than inner speech in a strict sense. For that matter *auditory imagination* is also broader than *inner speech* since one can imaginatively "hear" music, another person's voice, etc. But what I am after for the limited purpose of this paper is the linguistic thinking which I suspect is the on-going ordinary accompaniment of our experience.

Ordinarily we are so absorbed by our interests and our projects that we may fail to notice the linguistic structure of our thought. Spoken language "hides itself" in order to reveal that which it refers to. This can be shown by asking ourselves if we can hear our native tongue as "mere noise." I suspect it would be hard to attain this in experience—but it is not quite so hard to attain when listening to a strange tongue. But thinking, inner speech, auditory imagination, is so ultimate in our experience that it is even more hidden as language. Inner speech as an auditory imagination which is linguistic in structure is further hidden by its time structure. My thinking in this form is "faster," for example than my speaking—just as my speaking is much faster than my writing or typing. I suspect this accounts for both confusions over the relation of thought and language and for our frequent failure to notice the linguistic structure of our thinking.

One can begin to approximate directness even in this case when we employ the imaginative variations suggested by Husserl. For example, my thinking as an auditory imagination in language can be found to be English. This becomes apparent if I try to think in French or German—neither of which I do spontaneously—though I hope some day to be able to do so. Recently I asked a quadralingual person what language she used for thinking. Her answer that she alternatively thought in one of the four languages and added that this was in some ways a disability since she felt that even though she had four forms for thinking she was master of none.

This auditory imagination in the form of language displays certain characteristics which are common to other forms of imagination. For example, as with visual imagination I can vary the object of my thinking freely. Visually I can imagine a purple butterfly or a green cow; auditorily I can think about Plato's ideas or the voice of my wife. Moreover, no matter how brilliant my visual imaginations may be they are present as "irreal" for the object of imagination is distinct from the object of perception. In a similar way my inner speech or auditory imagination has the "irreal" presence which is distinct from the language I hear from another through a hearing perception. My auditory imagination is the unsounded correlate of my perceived or spoken language.

But just as visual and auditory perception differ, so are visual and auditory imaginations different. For example, I can turn my visual imaginations off and on at will just as perceptually as I can close and open my eyes. Visual images are not constant. This is clearly not so easily the case with auditory imagination. My "thinking" in this linguistic form accompanies my various activities. I suggest you try to "turn off" this thinking altogether.

To be sure, auditory imagination may from time to time "recede" just as sounds recede. I may be so engrossed with a given project that I fail to notice in any explicit fashion the presence of auditory imagination. But if I but ask after it and its presence it appears as immediately there. Thus just as I find it hard to isolate myself from the pervading presence of sound I find I cannot escape my auditory imagination or thinking.

Its presence varies with my attention; if I am concentrating on a philosophical problem it fills my consciousness; if I am cutting a tree down to add to my cabin it is present only on the fringes. But it is rarely absent and the only time it appears to be so in anything approximating a total way is when I change to the imagination of music rather than thinking. (One might note that in the German version of the arts music was classified as one of the *redente Künste*. Music would constitute a special problem for a phenomenology of the auditory.)

Further, this auditory language is often totally imageless. It may be accompanied by visual imagery, but it need not be. Ordinarily I "hear" myself think (note that in the presence of distracting noise we might well say: "quiet down, I can't hear myself think"). One could say in an almost Wittgensteinian sense that there is linguistic thinking were it not that I had a fairly high degree of control over this activity or that the presence of such thinking raises again the question of a transcendental age.

Further auditory imagination, just as perceived sound, displays the already discussed temporalistic structures. It is timeful, on-going, constant. Indeed, if described in detail it sounds very like the structure of consciousness described by Husserl. This pervasive presence of auditory imagination, "thinking," may well be a more primary mode of self-awareness than any other. I would only note that a visual image of myself is quite rare if not impossible. But my auditory self-awareness is usual and it is in a nonimagistic mode that I project my possibilities toward the world. But here I am getting off the track.

As auditory imagination in the form of thought language I find an imaginative accompaniment to my perceiving. Thus at least in this single case I must modify the perceptualist emphasis of phenomenology to say that *both* language and the perceived world are co-present. With Merleau-Ponty I would maintain that a complete reduction to a pure perception is impossible—but I would add that what is discovered at the limit of the reduction is the juncture of perception and language (as thought) in the co-presence of auditory imagination and the life-world of perception.

CHAPTER TWO

On Perceiving Persons

The puzzle of perceiving persons with its attendant problem of the relation between behavior and mental events has had a long history in Ordinary Language circles. One recalls Ryle's "ghost in the machine," the Wisdom-Austin symposium on "Other Minds," and Strawson's *Individuals*. Here, however, I wish to enter this discussion from a different perspective, a more phenomenological one, while adopting at least one implicit analytic strategy of displaying aspects of the problem not ordinarily supposed.

In reading the literature on this problem I am often impressed by what appears to me as a theory of experience which remains "disembodied" from its perceptual context. My first concern here is to point up certain aspects of perceptual and imaginative "embodiment," particularly as it occurs in the domain of spoken and heard language.

There is in phenomenology a concern for the understanding of intersubjectivity which gives special significance to *language*. For while it remains that "all our relations with the world are intersubjective," as Professor Ricoeur reminds us,[1] it is in language that my immersion in the intersubjective is most manifest. But one should note that when it comes to the ordinary situations in which one perceives persons it is *spoken language* which is the most explicit occasion of intersubjective appearing. In general one can say that I am present to myself, to others, and to the world within an already established, but open-ended context of meanings which are broadly language. And in this sense language

---

1. Paul Ricoeur, *De l'interprétation* (Paris: Editions du Seuil, 1965), p. 376.

transcends the artificial boundaries of consciousness and behavior. But more specifically the most explicit and primary manifestation of language is to be found within that which is spoken, within auditory experience. Here I must be wary, since this seems to be empirically contingent and since there are other than auditorily embodied "languages." But contingency is not to be dismissed lightly; rather it should be investigated for its relevance to how language is understood more generally. Again, my concern is to move away from a "disembodied" notion of language.

But to point this factor up I resort to a dramatic device (temporarily for the purposes of this paper). This device is the attempt to select auditory perception and imagination as the primary variable from an admittedly global perceptual experience and relate this "abstracted" variable to the problem of perceiving persons. In a sense this device is a counterfoil to what I generally believe is the predominance of visual examples and metaphors which occurs within philosophical discussion. From Aristotle on, the tendency has been to discuss perception through the paradigm case of the visual and the same goes for correlated discussions of the imagination. I shall argue that while not all discussions of visual perception and visual imagination are irrelevant, the tendency to concentrate upon the modes of *the seen* tends to obscure an area of phenomena which are extremely important for the problem of perceiving persons.

In my selective device I shall attempt to display an auditory dimension of experience which I believe in some respects lies closer to the problem of perceiving persons than the visual paradigm. I do not wish to prejudice the case against a fuller description of global experience, but I do wish within the limits here to re-balance the case in favor of auditory experience. The formula which shall guide this discussion is: *inner language is the imaginative auditory correlate to language as heard within the broader perception of sound.*

Negatively, the tendency to take visual perception and visual imagination as paradigms results in an overemphasis which may hide aspects crucial to the perception of other persons.

Within the phenomenological tradition this tendency to overempha-

---

2. Jean-Paul Sartre, *Being and Nothingness*, trans. H. E. Barnes (New York: Philosophical Library, 1956), pp. 252-301. It is true that Sartre uses the look in a broader than visual sense. In the example of the man surprised at the keyhole he first hears the other—but the descriptions are governed by the notion of presence by sight.

size the *seen* is apparent in Sartre's brilliant, but limited discussion of "the look." Sartre showed that the "look" can objectify me in the presence of another. When an other appears he rudely shakes me from my solipsistic presence to the world and my world "bleeds" away before his gaze. Merleau-Ponty moves toward correction of this overemphasis, which I am here laying at the door of a preoccupation with the seen, by pointing out that if the "look" objectifies me this remains the case only if I withdraw into my own thinking nature.[3] He further locates the embarrassment of the gaze as unbearable, "only because it takes the place of possible communication."[4]

Seeing the other is an occasion which places a further and higher demand upon me. I sit in my office typing a paper, hoping to finish it in time for a deadline. I am absorbed in my project when the door opens and a student walks in. His presence ruptures the preoccupation I had with my project, but I finish typing the sentence I had begun. But his presence not only breaks the relation with my project—it also places a demand upon me, a demand to recognize him and a *call to speak*. His general presence now takes explicit form in a communication through spoken words in a language which is common to both of us. His visual presence is the occasion for a call to speak. Further, I will best "perceive" what he wants through the explicit manifestation of speech.

By varying the situation to one in which speech is restricted, one heightens the embarrassment of a merely visually centered situation. Imagine the frustration I have in a country in which all others speak a language foreign to me. Here I have little idea about the other's "mental states" at all, but my frustration is not due to the poverty of the seen, it is due to a specific poverty within the heard. My puzzlement in this case is the auditory analogue to the oddness I experience in the presence of an object I cannot recognize. The other's observed body may not be strange, but the way in which his language is embodied is.

It is precisely this simple but usually unattended aspect of perception which calls for display. The problem of perceiving persons is as much and may be more centrally located in auditory perception than in visual perception. For if we are most manifestly related intersubjectively through language it is also the case that in its ordinary form that relation occurs within auditory experience and its modes.

---

3. Maurice Merleau-Ponty, *Phenomenology of Perception*, trans. C. Smith (London: Routledge and Kegan Paul, 1962), p. 361.

4. *Ibid.*, p. 361.

The auditory, however, is broader than perception in a narrow sense. There is both a perceptual and an imaginative "hearing" which are correlated in ways similar to visual perception and imagining. My "inner language" is to my speech and my hearing as my visual imagination is to my visual seeing and its objects. This is merely to point out that imagination has both an auditory and a visual mode. And there is special significance to auditory imagination and auditory perception in relation to the problem of other persons.

However, I should note that what I am calling "inner speech" and the auditory imagination is an exceedingly rich and varied phenomenon.[5] It would be very easy to get lost in the varied forms auditory imagination takes (for example: a debate with myself, the sheer association of scattered thoughts, concentrated effort in thinking). I am here concerned only with the very general nature of "thinking" as quasi-linguistic. I imaginatively "hear" myself thinking—or I think in terms of "speaking" language.

Turning to the phenomenon of inner speech, I find that in some sense I am aware of myself or present to myself as a constant ongoing "thinking" which has the irreal aspect of inner speech. This inner speech is the imaginative correlate of spoken language. In one sense this private awareness of myself is open only to me—no one may hear my inner language any more than they can see my visual imaginations. In this sense this auditory imagination is similar to visual imagination. It can also be varied at will and skip from subject to subject. Further, with visual imagination, it displays the irreal presence of all imagination. The "hearing" of this inner language is not hearing in the perceptual sense at all. It is the unsounded correlate of heard language which appears perceptually.

But in other respects auditory imagination or inner language is not symmetrical with visual imagination. For example, I cannot stop it at will, at best I can reduce it but for a moment. It does not go on and off as does visual imagination. It is true that I may have some difficulty being aware of my inner speaking, because it is not so obviously present if I am deeply engaged in some project. But this is in principle no different from any naive experience. Ordinarily the reference of experi-

---

5. This became quite apparent at the second workshop in phenomenology, June 1966, Washington University. Our investigations, under the direction of Herbert Spiegelberg, were directed towards soliloquy. Subsequent discussion revealed the complexity of the phenomenon.

ence is towards the project of that experience; intentionality is directed towards the world in phenomenological terms, but reflectively its presence may be detected. Inner speech goes on and I have but to notice it or try to suppress it and it becomes more obvious. (To notice it I may ask, "What language am I thinking in?" "Can I cease to think at all?") Indeed, this inner speech, this auditory imagination, displays many of the on-going temporal and voluntaristic aspects of the structure of the ego which phenomenologists describe.

I suspect if one expanded the point he might argue that this non-visual, auditory inner speech may be a more primary form of imagination than any other. I am ordinarily present within myself as inner speech—as language.

We now return to the problem of perceiving persons. I have argued that in the tendency to use the visual as a paradigm for most arguments about perception and imagination, many important dimensions of perceiving and imagining may be suppressed. Another person may well appear first within the visual field, but this appearance in the normal state of affairs is one of a call to speech. But speaking is part of the *heard* and auditory perception is the most explicit revelation of the other. Nor should this seem odd. If I am present to myself in terms of inner language, the imaginative correlate of auditory perception, why should not the other be most manifestly present to me through spoken language? His spoken presence is the perceptual correlate of my own presence to myself through imagination.

One can now push the explication further by paying attention to phenomena not ordinarily noticed in the perception of other persons. By joining the imaginative and the perceptual modes of the heard and situating them in the context of wider phenomena certain aspects emerge.

The importance of auditory imagination and perception is evidenced in the realm of person and self-perception. It is obvious that I cannot see myself as others see me because *I am* that which I wish to see. At best I see a few bits of myself.

This same difficulty is heightened in visual imagination. I suspect our visual imaginations of ourselves are exceedingly difficult and probably rare. Auditorily, however, there seems to be a parallel and a difference between self-perception and the perception of others. The parallel is found in that inner speech does not appear as the imagination of any other speaking. I may, of course, imagine another's voice and psychological studies seem to indicate that in certain types of schizophrenia even one's own inner voice takes on this characteristic. But ordinarily inner speech is more like actual speech in that I have difficulty experiencing it as if it were "heard" as others hear us. (Physically speaking, we *cannot* hear ourselves as others hear us since we hear our own voices by both ordinary hearing and through bone conduction. Our surprise at the mirror of a tape recording is warranted.) The difference is that the "self-perception" of inner speech is an almost constant I-activity. We might say that we are almost constantly present to ourselves in terms of this nearly ceaseless inner activity. In this sense I would hold our self-presence takes the form of auditory imagination.

The other, also, is perceptually present to me in a primary way through auditory perception. We are all familiar with the fact that we get to know someone much better by meeting him and talking to him over a long period of time. It is by language that I perceive more fully. One might almost say, as Walter Ong does, that vision objectifies and speech personalizes.[6] Or one might go on to suggest that language is that which spans both imagination and perception.

Of course in the broadest sense the explicit form of perceived speech is part of the larger phenomenon of sound and even here interesting notions are not lacking. I would suggest one final possibility. We often note that the presence of the other is "diffuse." Sartre speaks of Pierre's absence in this way.[7] But especially in conversation the presence of the other "surrounds us." We might even say, "I am absorbed in what he is saying."

Now if we sought to account for this seemingly disembodied presence with visual terms we might be tempted to say, "Nonsense—he is where his body is." But, interestingly enough, the same does not follow when we begin to notice the structure of sound. Sound, within which language occurs, surrounds us. It absorbs us and its location is never so precise, except in ideal situations, as that of a seen object. Sound, contrary to sight, *is embodied* or made present in this way.

Could it be that there is a connection between the presence of a person as "surrounding," "absorbing," as going beyond the bounds of

---

6. Walter Ong, Unpublished paper presented to the Technology and Culture Seminar at the Massachusetts Institute of Technology, March 7, 1966. The cases of writing and now modern "canned" communcations are interesting in themselves, but they are developments dependent upon spoken language.

7. Sartre, *Being and Nothingness*, pp. 278-79.

bodily presence and the similar presence of sound in general? Could it be that our preoccupation with the seen has been so intense that we have read it into and restricted our understanding of the perception of other persons so that we miss some of the concrete embodiment of the other in the world in the dimensions of sound? In characteristic phenomenological fashion I would only point out that our embodiment in the world is something that always needs "revealing." And the revelations of the other in and through the embodied presence of sound is particularly important for the problem of perceiving persons.

CHAPTER THREE

God and Sound

Merleau–Ponty's insistence upon the primacy of perception in the human life experience is suggestive for the thesis of this paper. *The most complex ideas within a given culture may contain implicit perceptual metaphors which in turn exercise a certain control over the development of those ideas.* The particular instance of this thesis which I wish to develop here is found in a parallelism between major general features of auditory phenomena and some of the major descriptive characteristics of the late development of God in the Bible, God in this case being considered as a cultural idea.

The general hypothesis upon which the particular thesis depends needs some initial qualification. (a) It should be apparent that any given culture is a complex and diverse entity, neither monolithic nor static in its being. Thus one would not expect to find any single model within the culture based solely and exclusively upon any single perceptual metaphor. The Bible, for example, makes varied references to visual appearances of God, an outrageous example of which is that of Moses viewing the "hindermost parts" of God while Moses was on the mountain. Visual metaphors, such as the "arms" or "wings" of God are also used. (b) But it is also the case that in a given cultural idea there is a discernible unity and a line of development which finds its expression in the establishment of a dominant tradition. This is in spite of the fact that recessive traditions may continue to exist and sometimes threaten to overthrow the dominant tradition. Thus, in the case at hand, in spite of the fact that the literature of Israel contains numerous references to the visualizability of God, the dominant tradition is one in which visual representations of God are absolutely forbidden. This tradition was apparently quite successful if one recalls the lack of fetishes, particularly in male form, in either archeological findings in Israel or in the construction of religious buildings. The Christian version of this prohibition finds echo in the claim of the New Testament that no man has ever seen God. But a break-down of the visual nonrepresentability of God occurs in Christianity as it moved into Greek culture where churches soon contained pictures or mosaics of God as an old man. This would have been offensive, at the least, to an ancient Hebrew.

By contrast, the Greek culture into which the tradition of the non-visualizable God moved, gloried in visualizable forms. Not only was it the case that the gods were portrayable, but one could argue the case that a predominance of a visual metaphor occurs in Greek culture and more particularly within philosophy itself. Not only did Aristotle claim that vision is the principal source of knowledge, but the use of visual metaphor in relation to rationality became a tradition itself. Thus the history of philosophy contains numerous visually derived terms for knowledge: "insight," *lumen naturale*, "clear and distinct ideas," and now *Lichtung*.

One could further argue that the epitome of visual predominance occurs in that offspring of Greek tradition, modern science. Here the very processes of measurement rely upon the ingenuity with which the investigator may construct spatializable and hence visualizable models for all other qualities. To measure is to know—but to measure is to make spatial and visual all that which is compared to the measuring standard.

In the parallelism here, however, it is the auditory metaphor in relation to the biblical God which shows an implicit perceptual metaphor. As a strategy I shall first isolate some features of auditory experience from the fabric of global experience in order to attain clarity. Then I shall turn to parallel features in the idea of God.

SOUND AS INVISIBLE

In its pure form sound is, strictly speaking, *invisible*. This may be merely to say that sound is not sight and is autonomously distinguishable from other forms of perception. But this initial negative characterization of sound presence perhaps needs to be made if we are to focus our attention upon the distinctive presence of sound for its own sake.

In global experience we speak of the sound of the violin or the sound of the waterfall. And in our speech we constantly use terms which may be confusing due to dual use ("clear sounds," or even "blue sound").

But sound has its own "bodily presence" in which its invisibility may even be helpful. For example, the full and complete presence of sound in listening to a symphony may be enhanced by the closing of the eyes. This is only one way in which we may concentrate our attention upon sound for its own sake. Note also that sound takes on more than usual significance against a background of darkness or the absence of light. In the dark we hear his footsteps and the blindman must rely upon and appreciate even more fully the significance of sound.

In the history of religion this situation also finds its forms in the records or tales of visions or experience of the divine. Not only do churches and synagogues often appear purposefully dark, but they frequently are made in such a way that echoes occur in odd ways. Indeed, one such classical vision is that of Isaiah in the Temple. Here it is precisely against the vagueness and darkness of a temple filled with smoke that God appears. It is only when He *speaks* that the vision begins to take on human significance. Phenomenologically, the dark, the vague, or the blind may be the visual background for the presentation of God in sound, i.e., in Word.

Note parenthetically that the invisibility of pure sound presents a problem for the scientific study of sound. It is when sound is reduced to or transformed into a visual pattern that it becomes scientifically intelligible. Thus oscillographs or Moire patterns, used to illustrate what sound must be like within a spatializable, visual pattern, are employed to make sound rational or measurable.

SOUND AS SPATIALLY SURROUNDING

This is not to say that sound is in itself non-spatial. But its peculiar form of spatiality is enigmatic precisely because the spatiality of sound is a *surrounding* spatiality. We are immersed in the world of sound—it is around us. Thus no matter how we turn our heads it still presents itself to us, unlike visual entities which can be made to disappear from sight by merely turning the head or closing the eyes.

Sound does present itself, in certain circumstances, as coming from a direction and we can tell where the source is and even to an extent the distance of the source. But in spite of this the sound itself "surrounds" us coming in both our ears and "invading" our being. Add to this the relative difficulty with which we may control sound intrusions as compared to sights. We must either exert great mental strength to shut out noise or must physically isolate ourselves from sound.

Again the parallel with the idea of God may be seen. Not only is God invisible or visually non-representable, but the biblical tradition speaks of the inability to escape from the surrounding presence of God. Even in Sheol He is present and the prophet in asking whether he may flee knows that there is no place from which to escape the surrounding presence of God. Thus metaphorically, just as we are always centered in a surrounding space of sound, so also does the Israelite think of God as encompassing his own being.

SOUND AS TEMPORAL

However, the essential characteristic of sound is perhaps its predominantly *temporal* nature. Normally sounds, unlike visually stable objects, constantly come into being and pass from it in a variable, temporal fashion. Thus, whereas the visual field usually displays a dominant number of stable objects against which motion occurs, with sound the stable or long lasting single sound is more likely the exception. The word of sound *is* a world of fury.

Note also that it is precisely on those occasions in which the visual field itself is unstable, as for example on the sea, that one must accustom himself to total motion. Contrariwise, it takes some effort to remain calm and stable in the face of a continuous single sound.

And if one were to turn for further collaboration of the essential temporality of sound one could note that a physics of sound indicates that our very ability to locate sounds depends literally upon the microseconds of time difference when a sound reaches our two ears. It might seem that this constant temporal variability of sound would keep it from becoming intelligible. But instead, temporality has become the basis for a central mode of soundful intelligibility. In its concrete form the use of sound in *speech* becomes a major item in the whole of man's rational (ordered) experience. Sound entities, if recognizable, are recognizable by their repetition in time. Thus with the song of the bird or the melody of the music the being of sound is "made to stand." It is speech in repeated and recognizable sounds which forms the main mode of intelligibility within the world of sound.

It is here that we begin to find a rich series of parallels between auditory phenomena and the nature of the Hebrew God. Historians of religion have long remarked upon the predominantly historical and temporalistic features of the Old Testament God. And at the same time we should take strong note of the fact that the primary way in which the Old Testament God manifested Himself was in Word.

The Old Testament God is recognizable by temporal repetition; He is the God of Abraham, Isaac, and Jacob, because he maintained his promise through time. No visual idol need be passed down from generation to generation, but the story, the telling, must be carried down through time. The God of the Old Testament is not timeless, but persistent through time.

Nor is He an abstract being since He is present to His people. But in what way? Primarily in terms of the agreement, the spoken covenant, between God and the people. It is in speaking to men that the Old Testament God manifests Himself. It is at this point that we should not only recall the strict prohibition placed upon visual representations of God, but note by contrast that *no* prohibition is placed upon His representations by means of Word. God speaks to His chosen, to the prophets and to Moses. If there is any correlate to the idols of the Canaanites it is to be found in the one visualizable way of representing living words, i.e., in the Torah as a written word. Thus if there is any corresponding problem of "appearance and reality" within ancient Hebrew culture it is to be found in the difference between the written word and its interpretation and the living-speaking word of God.

Thus the predominant form in which God appears is in terms of sound, in words. This is what contrasts biblical mysticism, for example, from other forms of mysticism. Here the peak of a religious experience is the reception of a word from God rather than of an identity between mystic and the divine. Here the relation is one of command to one commanded or of an argument between unequals, but always in relation to word. Even Job finally gets a word from the hidden God he struggles with, although it isn't the word he expected.

The intelligibility of the Hebrew God is parallel to the intelligibility of speech in terms of temporally repeated sounds. The God of Word is a God of time and sound. Or can we say that the experience of time and sound gives birth to the God of Word? In either case the parallelism is suggestive of the concrete place in which perceptual experience may be elaborated in the most complex cultural ideas and be directive of certain influences upon these ideas. The biblical God "hides" a perceptual metaphor which lies embedded in our auditory experience.

CHAPTER FOUR

Auditory Imagination

In this essay I propose to investigate phenomenologically a dimension of human experience which may be called *auditory imagination*. My central aim will be to point out certain phenomena which I claim properly belong to auditory experience and which, if so concretely located, are suggestive of solutions to some philosophical problems concerning man's experience of the world. I do not wish to claim that this investigation is either final or exhaustive, even in relation to the total range of auditory imagination. Certainly one result of phenomenological inquiry ought to be the rediscovery of the amazing wealth and complexity of human experience.

Methodologically I shall assume and employ some aspects of techniques known broadly as phenomenological. Thus my study will be descriptive and direct and I shall neither refer to already performed studies in overlapping areas nor to empirical studies upon the same phenomena. This is not to say that such studies are to be dismissed nor that they would not enrich this study.

Secondly, I shall begin with some very general features of the related phenomena of visual and auditory experience and move from these to the more specific range of phenomena within auditory imagination. In this context of a move from general to specific I shall employ the terms *field* and *entity* to distinguish the general from the specific.

Finally, I shall assume the primacy of the "normal," in a broad sense, over the deficient or the abnormal. The examples used here depend upon a fully conscious person complete with all his senses. Again this is not to say that variations by subsequent studies into abnormal or deficient subjects should be abandoned.

GENERAL FEATURES OF EXPERIENCE

Ordinary experience is global. We are so involved in our traffic with the world that we usually do not notice or reflect upon the way in which we experience the world. Phenomenology is one attempt to step back from certain types of involvement with the world and direct our attention to specific features of our experience of the world. Herein lies the clue to the epoché and the direction of phenomenological description. Thus while our original experience is global or total we can, nevertheless, isolate certain dimensions of that experience and submit them to descriptive scrutiny. Note here that it takes no apparent effort to experience things globally—but that it does take a disciplined effort to reduce global experience to any given dimension of that experience.

Reflective attention to experience, of course, has not been the total property of phenomenology and we find at hand many "latent" phenomenologies, some of which appear in rather ordinary philosophical and psychological distinctions. Beginning, then, with quite simple distinctions we may begin to look for some discoverable features of experience: (1) We shall first reduce experience by directing our attention to *visual* and *auditory* experience and isolate only some features of each dimension. (2) Note that from the beginning a pair of distinctions may be claimed within each dimension of experience. Two modes of experience, *perceptual* and *imaginative*, are possible for both visual and auditory dimensions. Husserl's "active" and "passive" syntheses are thus implicitly accepted here.

Given these preliminary distinctions we may begin by noting a limited number of general features of visual and auditory experience:

Visual and Auditory Field Phenomena: As field phenomena visual and auditory perception are constants of consciousness. To verify this we must pay strict attention to both dimensions strictly *as fields*, thus disrupting our ordinary attention which is involved with entities *within* the fields. In our ordinary affairs things are reversed and we are so involved with entities within the fields that, in "Heideggerian" fashion, we "forget" the field as a whole.

Thus if we close our eyes or enter a completely darkened room we might well say, "I can't see (any-*thing*)." Or, if the professor, drawing an X on the board, asks, "What do you see?" our response will likely be, "I see an X."

All of these responses, quite understandable if one assumes all the implied meanings of the ordinary context, would be wrong in relation to the fullness of field phenomena. Strictly speaking here we should say with eyes closed, "I see dull red," or something of that sort. With the blackened room we might say, "I see black," or "My visual field is completely black." With the X one might just as well go on to say, "I see an X; on a board; in a room; *within* a visual field." In each case there is a constancy to the field as "bodily present" so long as we are conscious.

The same constancy of the auditory field may be noted. The constancy of the *field* may be overlooked in instances which are auditory parallels with those of vision. The dark room parallel here is *silence*. We might be tempted to say, "I can't hear (any-sound)." Yet, though in this case it might be more unconventional, we might well say, "I hear the quiet." (I doubt that total silence is possible since in such surroundings one can usually hear his own heartbeat or the blood rushing in his ears.)

From silence to deafening noise, from blackness to blinding light the fields of vision and sound are constant. But our examples are also instructive about our experience as well. It is clear that we do not, nor could we, attend to the general features of perceptual fields in any regular way. We remain primarily involved *within* the fields, and there selectively. It may even be the case that we do not pay explicit attention to one or another field at a given time. If the visual and auditory fields are constant this is not to say that explicit attention upon them is constant.

It is here that we may note a more familiar feature of consciousness, often noted in phenomenological literature. Consciousness is directional, selective; it is *focused* as a "Husserlian ray." But if we relate the focus of consciousness to the constancy of the fields just noted we may speak of the focusing function as displaying a *core-fringe* structure. This is to say that we may attend to some particular entity within the given field in which case it constitutes the *core* of our attention while all else becomes *fringe*. Here, I suspect, we would need to add further observations about that which is implicit and explicit and that which is manifest and that which is latent if we were to go further with a study of the core-fringe structure of consciousness. For our purposes now note only that while attention constantly shifts (from one entity to another or by distraction by some striking intrusion into our project—such as a loud sound or bright light) it usually remains focused.

But this focus is itself *variable*. Visually I may attend to one object (core) while everything else becomes fringe; auditorily I may concentrate upon a single sound (core) and all else becomes fringe. But I may also expand the focus to a given set of objects (I scan the entire chess board; I listen to the whole symphony) while the fringe is unattended to (I don't attend to my opponent's chair; nor to the coughs of the audience). Here we could go on to note that selectivities differ as well. Thus while the "field texture" of the urban experience of sound tends to be quite loud the urbanite may easily hear the clink of a coin in the subway just as easily as the jungle dweller hears the faintest whisper of the adder amidst the parrot calls.

In both cases, however, *the directional focus* of the subject, which is a general feature of consciousness, *may obscure the phenomenon of the field itself*. It is only by reflective effort and by an expansion of focus to the field itself that the field emerges as open to investigation. Thus here within experience we find that one general feature may be obscured by another with the consequence that aspects of experience are easy to overlook.

But we return to features of the fields of vision and sound. If both are constant as fields within which a focus of attention may be operative, what distinguishes the fields as fields? The usual phenomenological answer would be to say that any field is distinguished by the characteristics of its "objects" (noema). Nor do I wish to quarrel with this insight since the visual features of visualizable entities (colors, etc.) are distinguishable from auditory features (pitch, etc.). However, field characteristics differ as well.

Kierkegaard's *Either/Or* suggested that sound, especially music, is temporal while that which is seen is spatial. This contrast which is suggestive for further phenomenological elaboration should not hide the fact that the auditory field is not solely temporal any more than the visual field is solely spatial.

The Space of Visual and Auditory Fields: Here we restrict our interest to the spatialities of vision and sound as field characteristics.

The spatiality of the visual field is a space *in front of* the subject. Moreover this space has the definite characteristics of being limited to a finite *roundness*. There is a border to my visual field and what is actually observed is always bounded by the "invisibility" of that which lies beyond. Here I may correctly say, "I do not see (beyond the roundness of my visual field)." Of course I may turn my head or eyes and see more of the world, present as anticipated, meant, or intended but not visually present outside my visual field. But even when I turn my head the visual field *as field* remains before me in its finite roundness. The space of the visual field is limited to being in front of me.

The spatiality of the auditory field displays a different character. It is clear that within the auditory field we may speak of the direction of a given sound (it comes from behind me) and of particular sounds we may perceive as being near or far from us. But as a field we must say that it *surrounds* us. I am immersed in the auditory field which displays no definite boundaries such as those of vision. The sound field, unlike the visual field which remains in front of me, displays an indefinite space in all directions from me. Note in passing that I may speak of myself at the *center* of auditory space. And note also that the indefiniteness of auditory space proceeds in both directions—it extends indefinitely from me but it also "invades" my being. (A physiologist once remarked that a well constructed theatre would present sound "in the middle of one's head.")

IMAGINATIVE EXPERIENCE

At this point, despite the fact that the general features of the visual and auditory fields are far from exhausted, we must begin some variations taken from the imaginative modes of visual and auditory experience. I do not intend here to enter the complex problems of the relationship of these two modes of experience other than to offer a tentative belief. It would seem, with Merleau-Ponty, that perception remains the primary, or at least the primitive mode of experience in which the world is presented to us.

Imagination, if restricted to "imaging," would seem to be dependent upon perception. Thus while one may imagine visually all sorts of imaginable animals they, like their perceptual counterparts, would still be colored and spatial.

However, there are ways in which imaginative activity, taken here as an "active synthesis" *exceeds* perceptual modes of experience. Further, there are variants within imaginative activity which make the activity quite distinct from perception and which raise some questions as to the primacy of perception.

Some General Features of Imaginative Activity: When we speak of imagining something one general characteristic of this human activity immediately emerges. All imaginative activity allows a free variation of its contents. Thus while in the imagination of fantastic animals it may be impossible to void the imaginative field of color characteristics it is possible to imagine blue centaurs or green griffins such as have never been perceived and thus "make possible" their perceptual appearance in statuary or pictures. Free variation of contents remains one general feature of imaginative activities not possible for the "passive synthesis" of perception except within limits (recall the famed ambiguous pictures of duck-rabbits which may be varied at will).

But first as a variation upon the general features of visual and auditory perceptual fields, do imaginative activities display the same general features? For example, are the visual and auditory imaginative fields constants of consciousness? Here the field phenomena are more difficult to describe even than in the case of the much more familiar perceptual fields. The reasons for the greater difficulty may be varied. We may remind ourselves that just as attention is focused within a perceptual field, so it is within imagination. And this to the extent that a given dimension may be obscured (perceptually I am so intent upon the picture that I fail to notice my wife calling me or imaginatively I am so intent upon my transparent pegasus that I fail to note the black background against which he is etched) by the focus.

I also suspect that imaginative activity in general is more difficult to deal with because it has something to do with the very way in which we are present to ourselves. Nonetheless, there are variations which may help display our thinking-imaginative fields. The old challenge, "Try *not* to think of a white bear," is an entity version of a possible field question, "Can you 'turn off' your thinking altogether?" I suspect that the answer must be a qualified "No." If so then some form of imaginative activity remains constant in consciousness just as the perceptual fields do. Consciousness may be consciousness of _____, never contentless, directed as phenomenologists claim, but it is also complex in the sense that its modes are multidimensioned.

To plunge into the totality of a thinking-imaginative activity is to enter a world too complex for immediate clarity. We must remain within the reduced limits of visual and auditory imagination—but even here there is more than enough to occupy us. In what form is imaginative activity a constant? We have not yet arrived at a clear display of the fields of imaginative activity, but now suspect that imaginative activity does display itself with some constancy even though that constancy may often remain at the fringe.

Further variations without restrictions may be suggestive. And here I wish to make two claims concerning visual imagination which may at first appear strange. (1) Not all the structural characteristics of the perceptual dimension carry over to the visual imaginative parallel, and this in regard to their respective fields. My claim is that *the field space of visual imagination is similar in structure to the field space of auditory perception and not to the field space of visual perception.* The field space of vision is in front of the subject; but the field space of sound surrounds the subject. Thus for an entity to appear visually it must be in front of the subject or the subject must turn in such a way that it comes in front of him. But for a sound to be present to a subject it may be anywhere and even fill the surrounding space.

Now turn to a fantasy variation within visual imagination: I may visually imagine a small red horse galloping on the floor behind me (of course I can also imagine myself seeing the horse there but this is merely to restate that imagination is *not* a perception). I seem to be able to place the visually imagined object in any position in relation to the *surrounding* imagined space. And if this is possible—let each try for himself—then the space of visual imagery parallels in at least one aspect the space of the auditory field and not its visual counterpart. In this sense the imaginative activity "exceeds" structurally its perceptual base.

(2) A second oddity of visual imagination as such appears to be possible. Visual imagination may be "turned off" or "turned on" in a way not possible for the field of visual perception. Here I am claiming that one may not only "turn off" certain contents, but may turn off the imaginative field entirely *as a field*.

Perceptually, of course, we may open and shut our eyes and thus easily control the contents of what appears to us. But as we noted, this merely changes the character of the field without removing the field. If there is any parallel within visual perception to the absence of a field it comes not from the easy closing of eyes, but from the absence of the field entirely beyond the finite roundish boundaries of my vision.

(I would but recognize in passing that the imaginative habits of given persons may vary quite differently. But these variations of actual habit do not establish structures or limits of any given mode of experience as such.)

AUDITORY IMAGINATION

Do these same variations occur within the auditory dimension of imagination? Here at last we arrive at the primary topic of investigation and here at last we shall note both some general characteristics and some more specific features of this mode of experience.

As a field phenomenon auditory imagination apparently displays the same general features that its perceptual base does, i.e., imagined sounds may be presented as coming from any direction or may surround the subject. Again the space of auditory imagination is *surrounding*. Note however that while the imagined sound may ordinarily be accompanied by visual imagery it need not be. An imagined sound may be "disembodied."

Thus there is lack of surprise in the case of auditory imagination in regard to the similarity of perceptual and imaginative spatial structure. But a second feature of auditory imagination, if it is normative, is more interesting. *Auditory imagination, unlike its visual counterpart, is almost always continuous.* At first this may seem too extravagant a claim, but since the claim depends upon noting several other facets of auditory imagination it may be well to wait until more evidence is in. Recall for the final time the difficulty posed by the focused attention in obscuring field or specific structures of experience. In the specific phenomenon I shall describe this is of greater than usual difficulty since the "thinking activity" itself tends to be involved with focusing itself.

With this warning in mind we may turn to variations within auditory imagination which will help isolate the specific phenomenon I have in mind. (1) It is immediately clear that auditory imagination displays the free variation of contents possible in all forms of the imagination. I may imagine, with or without visual imagery, voices of all kinds, an argument between two or more persons, noises of all types, music, etc. Further, the range of sound, from silence to deafening roar parallels the auditory perceptual range. (2) This free variability allows a certain "control" over contents not possible in the perceptual mode. Thus while I may, within limits, select out certain sounds among others perceptually I remain limited to the "passive synthesis" which does not depend solely upon my efforts. For example, if I am listening to an actual symphony I may focus upon the strains of the oboe and make them "stand out" from the background of the full orchestra—but only within limits since I may fail to hear the oboe when it is covered over by the blare of the French horns. In imaginative fantasy, however, I present myself with the sounds in such a way that my control is "active." This is not to deny that it is also possible to put myself in a receptive mood and merely allow sound images to present themselves as they will.

But these variations do not evidence auditory imagination as continuous since any particular instance of imagined sounds may be "turned off." But these images do not exhaust the active synthesis of imaginative activity and it is to a narrower and more specific range of phenomena that we must look if we are to locate the form of continuity of auditory imagination.

AUDITORY IMAGINATION AS INNER SPEECH

The phenomenon I have in mind is that form of "thinking" which may be called *inner speech*. I believe this ordinary, though not properly investigated activity, properly belongs to auditory experience in its imaginative mode. But to locate it properly several variations call for attention: (1) Inner speech is *linguistic* in character. We "think" in a language. Yet even this observation may go unnoted and for good reasons. First, we think *about something*. Once again our focus is directed in such a way we do not attend to the form of our experience in thinking. But also inner speech is a linguistic activity of extraordinary speed. It is a faster "speech" than actual or spoken speech.

Yet if we are asked simply, "What language do you think in?" we are quite quick to reply, "Why, English, of course." The importance of a native language becomes even more clear when we set about learning a second language. For example, a common phenomenon in learning a second language is that of *inner translating*. In seeking to say something in a second language at first I have to translate "inside my head." It is only much later and after much struggle that I learn to "think" in a second language. I have been told by experienced language instructors that even in the cases in which they are able to think in a second language it is usually the case that there remains a clearly primary and secondary language. Modern techniques such as "total immersion" which attempt to short-circuit inner translating are thus suggestive on several counts.

Even if we are now ready to accept the linguistic character of thinking this leaves us short of adequate evidence of its place in auditory imagination and short of establishing the almost constant presence of auditory imagination. But let it be clear here that the claim that inner speech is a normative mode of thought does not mean that thinking is exhausted by inner speech. There are too many obvious phenomena which cannot be included within an inner linguistic activity (such as the occurrence of "gestalt" insights, the "Aha!" phenomenon, in which a concept may only later be said. But even here it must be *said* if it is to become intelligible for someone else.)

(2) We may come closer to the needed location if we note a reverse variation. Is it possible to "turn off" one's inner speech? And if so under what conditions? It remains clear that the same shifting focus within a train of thought that is possible for any mode of consciousness occurs here. I may think along any given line; be interrupted and start off on another line; I may purposely abandon my thought and go on to something else. But may I turn off my thinking altogether? This is much less likely save in certain special situations.

A momentary "turn off" may occur in types of *shock* experiences. A loud sonic boom or a blinding flash of light may momentarily so shock me that my "thought is lost." But such shocks or disruptions remain momentary and usually succeed only in starting off a new line of thought. Intense shock, however, disrupts not only thought but perception as well and the blank look of a person in shock indicates an abnormal discontinuity to consciousness itself.

There are, however, less startling perceptual occurrences which hold a special position in the disruption of inner speech and these are to be found in auditory experience. The suggestion of their importance is contained in the saying, "It's so loud that I can't hear myself think." Noise, in filling the surrounding space of auditory perception "invades" my being and in particular my thinking self. Control here is difficult short of stuffing my ears or actual removal of my presence from the source. This lack of control over auditory presence and the invasion of my very self was well recognized recently by a company perfecting riot control instruments. The most effective instrument, they claim, is a high pitched directional sound which "hurts" the hearer even with his fingers in his ears. In the case of vision one may easily shut his eyes or divert his head to close off the offensive spectacle. With auditory perception control tends to be "psychic." Thus the teen-ager seems to be able to do his homework to the noise of folk-rock. Yet it remains the case that if serious or concentrated thinking is to be done it is usually the quiet place that is sought. Auditory perception intrudes into thought much more directly than visual phenomena.

(3) But if perceptual experience may disrupt a given chain of thought it is much more likely to merely set it off in another direction. The same is the case with visual imagination. It is quite possible to either attend to

a set of visual images or to let them come as they will, and some persons evidently have a more constant procession of images than others, but at the same time one may continue to "think" in the form of inner speech. Is this possible with auditory imagination? In this case it seems possible, for the first time, to *replace* inner speech. But it is replaced with an auditory phenomenon such as imagined music. Thus in both cases it remains that auditory experience is that dimension of experience which relates to, intrudes upon, or replaces inner speech. But it also remains the case that there is a certain constancy to one or another form of auditory experience.

In the attempt to locate a quite common and perhaps predominant form of thinking, inner speech, within the realm of auditory imagination we have so far attended to variations upon the broad spectrum of general auditory phenomena. A further set of variations, remaining within auditory phenomena, is also possible. In this case let us note several comparisons between spoken speech and inner speech. (4) Let us first restrict ourselves to some facets of speech for a single subject. It is the case, for example, that I hear myself speak. But this phenomenon usually remains upon the fringe while the core of attention is placed upon what I want to say, upon "putting my thoughts into words" or as in this case one might say, "putting inner speech in spoken speech." (It is also the case that one may "think out loud" in which case one merely "lets out" a free association of words much as one may allow images to flow before in imagination.) It is here that we note once again the relative speeds of spoken and inner speech. A part of the effort in speaking is directed towards saying what one is thinking but frequently falling short of the mark. I find that I have not said all that I have thought in a way similar to the note taker who cannot, because he does not have the skills of shorthand or speed writing, capture more than an outline of a lecture. And since there is, to my knowledge, no comparable way to transcribe the faster speed of inner speech into spoken speech and remain intelligible—the lag remains. Literary attempts to capture the "stream of thought," even the excellent ones of a James Joyce, remain reconstructions rather than transcriptions.

But the secondary feature of spoken speech also contains some interesting features. When I hear myself speak I am at one and the same time the speaker and the recipient of the speech and so long as I remain in this double role I cannot hear myself as another hears me. Thus when I am placed in the second role, by means of a tape recorder for example, it is not unusual to say, "That doesn't sound like me," since I have not before heard myself apart from *being* the speaking subject. Of course I may *learn* to recognize myself in the same way that a child learns to recognize himself in the more familiar mirror.

In other words, the sound of my speech is never heard first as "out there" as "coming from another source" but remains primitively related to the primary phenomenon of my focused activity in speaking. My primary focus obscures or covers over other features of my speaking. The same phenomenon occurs in inner speech but with greater obscurity. When I think (linguistically) my effort is upon the problem or project at hand. I am the subject thinking primarily, although I may secondarily recognize that I am using language in doing this. But it remains the case that thinking is *my* activity. Hence my inner speech, just as my spoken speech during the actual time of its occurrence, does not and cannot appear to me as "coming from elsewhere." Rather it remains primitively identified with the thinking activity itself. This means that there is necessarily a phenomenological distinction between the representation of an imagined voice of someone else coming from somewhere and the imaginative presence of my inner speech. But both presences remain imaginative activities of free variation and both, I believe, properly belong to *auditory* imagination. Of course we must recognize that my inner speech, under normal circumstances, can never appear to me as a voice coming from elsewhere since there is no instrument capable of capturing it for me. (Some disruption, such as a psychosis, may perform this. In such an abnormal case, however, it is quite likely that hidden in the mystery of the body there is something "physically" askew.)

(5) Note finally that inner speech as an auditory phenomenon in the imaginative mode may again portray a general feature of auditory space. In concentrated thinking, for example, thought in the form of inner speech may appear to *fill* the consciousness. I am "engrossed in" my thought; it surrounds me—just as auditory space surrounds me and may, in the striking sound of a symphony, fill my being.

Inner speech, then, as a very important facet of the thinking process and probably the central form of that process, displays the features of an auditory imagination. It is a free variation which presents itself as *my* activity in the form of language. It ranges from a fringe phenomenon in the cases of concentrated efforts upon projects in the perceptible world to a core phenomenon in the cases of concentrated thought. Its "spatiality" is that of auditory space which is or may be surrounding and which may or not be accompanied by other forms of imagination. And it is this visually imageless or latently visually imageless activity which presents itself as its own type of totality which remains an almost constant dimension of experience.

SUMMARY

At the end of this preliminary and at best suggestive essay it is perhaps appropriate to acknowledge that to this point I have not gone beyond a phenomenological psychology which itself remains incomplete. I would, however, like to suggest that the suggestions of such a phenomenological psychology may hold some significant clues to philosophical problems. Thus before leaving the area of auditory phenomena as one important dimension of our experience of the world I should like to indicate a few areas in which just such a phenomenological analysis may be of use: (1) It is not without consequence that a seeming predominance of visual metaphors has been used in the history of philosophy even in relation to our thinking activities. Phenomenology as well has frequently relied upon visual metaphor to describe such activities (*Wesensschau, Sicht, Abschattungen*, etc.) Yet visual metaphors, if inner speech constitutes any important dimension of thought, are inadequate to the phenomena themselves. (2) Already implicitly recognized but not investigated either here or elsewhere with sufficient study is the relationship between our experience of time and auditory phenomena. It is not without reason that Husserl should have used musical occurrences to illustrate the inner time consciousness. (3) In a different area the insistence of analytic philosophers upon the privileged position of language as a philosophical problem is not without merit. If, concretely, inner speech as an almost constant auditory imagination is to be understood as language, then the relationship of language to perception, for example, needs much further examination. (4) The currently much discussed problem of other persons also should relate to an examination of auditory phenomena. In spite of the fact that in this discussion much is often made of how we might be fooled by a good robot the predominant way in which we come to recognize and understand another remains linguistic in the quite concrete phenomena of speech (and secondarily in writing which is a visual derivate). For example, if I am present to myself in thought which has the form of language this remains an imaginative inner presence, that has its perceptual counterpart in the speech I hear of the other. Thus in this case language becomes the intersubjective appearance of the other to me and of my innermost thoughts to myself.

The essay, at least, represents a call for further investigation of auditory experience and the role it plays in our experience of the world prior to too quick conclusions about higher functions of human speculation. It is latently a call for a full phenomenology of sound within the limits of a Husserlian "regional ontology."

CHAPTER FIVE

Listening

The researches which lie at the origin of this essay were conceived of in a seminar on the phenomenology of perception in which auditory experience was to be of particular importance. The aspect of auditory phenomena we choose to describe here relates to a phenomenology of listening to music. The problems which arose in approaching music revealed interesting questions about comparative types of phenomenological methods.

In brief, the task of attending to music began to show a difference in emphasis between the use of "Husserlian" as compared to "Heideggerian" phenomenologies. In the Husserlian version the emphasis is upon positive attention to the phenomena. This positivity, described in the literature as the "ray of attention," "focusing," etc., gradually betrayed more and more basically visually derived metaphors as the favoured means of getting at experience. In contrast, the Heideggerian emphasis upon "letting be," the insistence that the phenomenon "manifest itself from itself" could be described as a negative means of attaining what is sought for by a process of gradually excluding irrelevant factors. An auditory metaphor lies behind this version of phenomenological reduction.

We shall seek here both to increase the contrast of methods and to describe the results by which we found a Heideggerian approach more and more appropriate to the problem of listening to music. Several words, however, are in order concerning the context of the seminar. First, it was presumed from the the basis of the prior research that the investigation of auditory experience, particularly when compared to studies and illustrations from visual experience, was a relatively underdeveloped field of inquiry and examples. We found through an investigation of the literature in relation to psychological experiments in perception that this generalization was clearly supported. Secondly, the use of visual metaphors in the language often tended to create a tradition of interpretation which, in the Heideggerian sense tended to hide or "cover over" (even the Heideggerian use is often visual in its metaphors) the phenomena. Thus as a device by which traditional assumptions and interpretations could be located and possibly removed, the seminar proposed to attempt descriptions which would at least point up the use of visually related terms or at most to use a language which would avoid such terminology.

Both these warning factors are, of course, related to a type of phenomenological reduction whose purpose is to remove assumptions and presuppositions but not to reduce experience. The phenomenological reduction is supposed to clear the field for description. The steps of this process and the attendant problems are reported below.

EPOCHÉ: ORDINARY EXPERIENCE AS THE LEVEL OF CLICHÉ

First attempts at description without instruction or carefully worked out approximations are frequently frustrated due to the tendency of mere description to yield *traditions.* In the case of music such traditions include the use, as description, of both previously formulated conceptual schemas and ordinary common sense comments. "I hear an octave," or, "that is a chord composed of $A^{\#}$ and F," are examples of statements which may mistake a conceptual classification for direct description. "That is a loud noise," or "That's screechy," are examples of the ordinary response prior to phenomenological reduction.

This state which is usually the result of pre-phenomenological demands for description corresponds to the problem of the "natural attitude" in the Husserlian context. Mere description confuses categories and may do so to the extent that a classificatory scheme is taken as the phenomenon itself (a similar case of such confusion exists when persons say, "I see images on my retina"). Thus a clearly directive question must be posed and posed in such a way as to give shape to the inquiry. In Husserlian terms the "natural attitude" must be replaced by a "phenomenological attitude." This displacement is the framing of a question addressed to the phenomena in question.

But this is also to say that the phenomena do not just "speak out" themselves—they "speak to" a question addressed them. One's *project* sets the context and is already a preselection concerning what may occur within the context. In this sense and to this degree epoché is also interpretation, but the more serious question is one which concerns the significance or additional yield possible through this interpretation.

The framing of the question, however, may be understood in at least two ways. In the Husserlian emphasis the direction is one which seeks to *focus* attention upon the phenomenon. This is a matter of placing limits upon other aspects of experience in order to concentrate upon that which is sought. The Heideggerian emphasis is, to a certain extent, an inversion of the former insofar as the gaining of the phenomenological position is one which successively opens one to the emergence of the phenomena "from themselves." However, in the early stages of the descriptive process both methods require a set of progressive reductions toward the phenomena. In the Husserlian interpretation this is the progressive bracketing of presuppositions; in the Heideggerian hermeneutic it is the gradual loosening up of calcified interpretations.

PHENOMENOLOGICAL REDUCTIONS: RE-LOCATING DESCRIPTIONS IN ORDER TO GET TO UNNOTICED ASPECTS OF THE PHENOMENON

The first steps in getting to the phenomena turn out to be directed away from immediate experience and towards making interpretations stand out in such a way that their distinction from the phenomena become evident. This is already implied in the failure of *mere* description. In the case at hand the pointing up of conventions about auditory phenomena which use visual metaphors provided the vehicle for this separation of phenomenon and interpretation. We found, as one might suspect, that these traditions are so integrally bound to our ordinary descriptions of auditory experience that we take that experience for granted without seeing how or whether our descriptions are justified.

In the language *about* auditory experience we found an abundance of (visually) spatial terms. Sounds are "movements," there is "up" or "high" and "down" or "low," etc. More significantly in relation to music, we noted that in musical theory and musical training the conceptual scheme is again one dominated by visual metaphor. For example, one is trained to conceive heard impressions as "distances intervals" or a "leap" of an octave, and musical notation (in the Western tradition at least) has rationalized a conceptual scheme which is thoroughly based upon spatial analogues. All of this may be noted without ever inquiring into experience. The phenomena have not yet "spoken" to either confirm or negate the conventions about them. But in making ourselves self-conscious about the traditions as traditions a question begins to take form in relation to the experiences we were after.

Is it self-evident that "movement" is a primary phenomenological characteristic of music presence? Is musical experience "spatial"? What does experience "show"? Or, if the answer confirms the visual-spatial characteristics of the experience of music, how does this occur? Methodologically, now, we are at the juncture where the comfortable assumptions afforded by ordinary awareness are called into question and the phenomenological shift is one which demands that experience "speak" in a new way. We are aware, of course, that this shift is one which purposely and "violently," if we use the Heideggerian notion, displaces the familiarity of the ordinary.

Once the conventions concerning music are called into question the experience of listening must be described from the implied "new" basis. In our first investigations it did not seem that spatial characteristics were integrally related to musical presence at all. Music's "movement" does not occur spatially. Its mode of presence carried its own uniqueness. But at the same time we found that a description which would totally avoid spatial imagery was difficult if not nearly impossible. Here, although we found the usual frustration of phenomenologists regarding the "limitations" or "restrictions" of language to be apparent, we also found that a re-arrangement of spatial considerations helped to point up unnoticed characteristics. Thus as we begin our descriptions we note that we remain "conservative" in the sense that we do not attempt a total rejection of the dominant visual-spatial imagery. What follows is a series of examples, "perspective variations," which lead us ever more deeply into Heideggerian notions in relation to listening.

One place in which the greatest "distance" between the direct experience of listening to music and the classificatory scheme seemed to appear was in some of the relations between the Occidental notational system and the experience of what is heard. In this classificatory scheme the octave serves as a basic unit which, in its visual model, shows the interval of the octave as the greatest distance and all other intervals expressed as lesser distances.

But auditorily the case is quite different. To hear an octave the two notes which frame the octave are present as "close" or having no sense of "movement" or "space" between them. Distance in terms of conflict, for example in atonal combinations, would seem more appropriate for "distance" notations.

But this is too "conservative" because the mere re-arrangement of the spatial metaphors also shows its inadequacy. Again, in relation to bass figurations "wide" intervals are often used and the octave is frequently one of these. Yet in listening this "jumping" is not a dominant characteristic of the bass line—it is heard as a "smooth" undergirding of the music and is comfortably integrated into it.

In fact, one must be thoroughly trained to recognize the "spatial" characteristics of sound. Initial listening exercises disclose that one does not naturally hear an interval as a given "size" or "distance." The association of the space of a fifth, a sixth, a third, with the appropriate sounds is learned. And even after some degree of training it is possible to mistake a fifth for an octave and it is often difficult to tell whether an interval moves "up" or "down." The spatial scheme is associated with— or perhaps imposed upon—the experienced sound. Here the temptation in ordinary description to confuse the music with its notation is much like the linguistic problem of confusing language with its reference. The distance between the notational system and the experienced sound is in fact complicated by a third factor. A total musical theory lies at the base of musical notation and in our tradition that theory is one which from the Greeks is based upon mathematical interpretations of musical phenomena. Thus hidden between the notation which often gives up our spatial metaphors concerning experienced sound and the experience of sound is a vast schema of "mathematizing thought."

But it is time to turn more directly to noted characteristics of listening to music. One of the first aspects which began to stand out in relation to this phenomenon was the *fragility* of the musical phenomenon. Within the global field of auditory phenomena, sounds of all types are present. This very fact complicates and acts to the detriment of musical presence. It becomes impossible, in ordinary contexts, to secure an exclusive focus upon music because of the global presence of sound.

From the Husserlian interpretation this failure of total focus might raise some questions about the possibility of even getting to "the things themselves." But from a Heideggerian interpretation other things may be noted. For example, imagine a living room in which a stereo set is playing. By first attempting to concentrate as exclusively as possible upon the music we become aware that a manifold of other noises *intrude* upon this project. Our very project makes these noises explicit in such a way that from their previously ordinary presence we now discover they have been implicit. The focus of attention upon the music makes the other noises appear as distractions—but they also stand out in more vivid fashion. In attempting to listen to music for itself we become more rather than less sensitive to introducing noises. As purists each minor distraction becomes apparent, each scratch, each external noise distorts the music itself.

This fragility of music increases in direct proportion to the concern of attention "toward" it—and paradoxically the fringe noises of the environment begin to benefit from the attention towards music presence. Auditory phenomena *intrude* into my awareness. This specific experience, however, also begins to point up a more general feature of auditory experience. In our familiar immersion in a sound world we live with sounds that pass for the most part unnoticed as the iceberg which passes mostly submerged.

What is to be noted concerning the above phenomena is that the previously submerged noises do not intrude as a result of gesturing "toward" them. In the auditory realm our focusing, which should effect an exclusion, negates itself and produces the contrary effect of increased vulnerability in an increased openness to the environment's total presence. Not content with the situation, we begin to notice a series of exercises designed to correct the problem. These exercises, which may be called the "Shh—be quiet!" phenomenon, begin to indicate the direction of auditory gesturing.

For example, if one wishes to itemize the auditory environment a positive act is one which gradually or suddenly calls for more and more quietness. One gestures "away from" sound "towards" silence. And the more effective this gesture-direction becomes, the more one realizes silence, the more radical the intrusions of formerly unobtrusive auditory disturbances become. The penultimate case occurs when one enters a well constructed anecho chamber which has been so built as to eliminate sound reverberations. He finds that two tones *intrude* into auditory consciousness, one higher than the other. The physiologist will tell the observer that one is the flow of the blood stream and the other the "current" in the nervous system—both of which had been unnoticed and unheard before.

Of course, to hear best one calls for relative silence. Nor is it simply a matter of receptivity. Lecturers and actors on occasion speak softly for emphasis and the most arresting sound is often subtly minimal as the "still small voice" of the biblical God. This arresting characteristic of soft sound approximates or is a gesture towards *silence*. The concentrated atention-direction of listening is a gesture towards silence.

Artificial devices, earphones for stereo music, heighten this aspect of listening. Earphones do not so much make the music better as they shut out extraneous noise—this device enhances the sound of music by securing an accompanying silence. Gesturing towards silence enhances listening.

Here the Heideggerian model again makes its appearance. The horizon of sound is silence, but at the same time it is the "absence" which is never attained. To suggest that silence is the primordial ground of music may seem abstract at first—but we contend that the gradual realization of this aim for listening may sharpen the listening experience. Silence is the unspoken background for sound.

It is here that one may begin to return to the problem of language in relation to the descriptive attending to music. Silence is the "space" of music. The "motion" which occurs in music is the motion through silence. In (visual) space, movement is a matter of displacement, relocation, or "matter" which is always someplace, comes from someplace, and goes somewhere. In music sounds come "from silence" and "return to" silence.

This is not to say that the coming-into-being and passing-from-being of sound is irrational. For example, in listening to music one begins to anticipate the expected sounds. There is a desire to hear additional tones and for those tones to be well related to those before. But our concern is never whether or not there is "room" for that tone. Here we reach one possible rationale for the appeal of music. In the musical world as perhaps in no other it is possible to create something from nothing.

Even the listener in the case of the recorded piece has the possibility of rejecting the music by lifting the arm of the player. In this act lies the power to make a particular strain of sound stop. But higher in the scale of creation lies the sheer potentiality of silence. Through the creation of music man can manipulate the mysteries of being and becoming, of actuality and potentiality, and through the vehicle of music man can legislate the schedule of a phenomenon's passage from its total being to its absolute annihilation. In the tones of music the "matter" of sound waxes and wanes at the player's discretion. And when it passes there is no residue. The conservation of matter or energy does not apply here. At base this coming-to-be from silence from which music stands out shows the "space" silence of sound as possibility. Silence is nothingness but nothingness is sheer possibility. This Heideggerian expansion from musical phenomena is one which in turn points back to that methodology. In the Heideggerian model with its concepts of "call," "silence," and the "voice (of conscience)" the fundamental thinking which occurs is a thinking with roots in auditory metaphor. And to follow the implications and pathways from that metaphor as a shift from the traditional visual metaphors of our philosophies may open a new direction for Western thought.

CHAPTER SIX

Parmenidean Meditations

Being is complete on every side, like the mass of a well-rounded sphere, equally balanced in every direction from the centre. —Parmenides

Most commentators from ancient times have held that Parmenides the Eleatic made a decisive step in the history of philosophy which led to the severing of our perceptual experience from our conceptual experience. This interpretation of Parmenides is based upon the enigmatic statements of Parmenides about his perfect sphere of being, full, immovable, and timeless. Surely, the commentators argued, nothing could be farther from the evidence of the senses. Therefore, Parmenides must have been talking about a pure conceptual realm to which the sense must be sacrificed when they contradict the certainties of the conceptual.

Phenomenology, particularly in its post-husserlian forms, has moved in a counter-direction. Its observations upon experience in its concrete forms have more and more called into question the tradition which severs concept from percept. Could it be that phenomenology has re-discovered something Parmenides may have known? And, if so, could it be that the traditional interpretation of Parmenides is wrong?

Could it be that Parmenides was a much more profound observer of experience than his critics and commentators were? Could it be that Parmenides was *both* right in his interpretation of the sphere of being *and* that his interpretation of being is also a description of the *field* of perceptual experience?

My purpose here is to begin with a re-interpreted Parmenides as a background figure against which to pose some observations about auditory experience understood phenomenologically. But a circle beginning with Parmenides which then moves to auditory experience and then returns to Parmenides cannot be closed too quickly. The ways of Parmenides and of phenomenology are not those of common sense. Thus I begin by setting a context in terms of history and method; then I trace certain aspects of auditory experience; and finally return to a parmenidean summary of Sound.

PHENOMENOLOGY AND AUDITORY EXPERIENCE

In scanning both philosophical and psychological literature it seems that the area of auditory experience is at least relatively underdeveloped. Philosophy, particularly, seems to have a primary visual orientation in its metaphors and models for thought and reality. This in spite of the fact that the auditory dimension is so important, perhaps centrally important, in our thinking and speaking insofar as it is tied to concrete language.

Perhaps one reason for this underdevelopment lies in the very familiarity of closeness of thought as language to us. Heidegger has pointed out well that that which is closest to us is the most difficult to note and thought as language is one of these phenomena. Its very intentionality as it refers to something else makes it invisible to itself. To note it we must make indirect and reflective studies. And today we have several such types of study. The empirico-linguistic studies "objectify" language. They make it into an "object" or a model which has hypothetical characteristics which can then be observed in operation (and in the process the concrete operators, experiencing persons, are either ignored or reduced to quasi-mechanical figures). On the other side are the phenomenologists who insist upon leaving the operator inside the equation and who attempt to thematize language reflectively as an experience process.

But language is only one part of auditory experience. Music, the problem of silence, auditory hallucination, all are included in auditory experience. I shall allude to each of these features in the survey to follow.

While it is certainly the case that for phenomenologists a brief note on method will be elementary, it is perhaps well to be aware of the general aim of our "reduction." (A) Husserl called it getting "to the things themselves" or, as it later became known, as reaching towards the level of pretheoretical experience. (B) To gain this level of experience we are called upon to lay aside or suspend our usual traditions of interpretation to the extent that the "objective" world as a judgment is laid aside.

But epoché, easy to describe, is not easy to practice because our natural and traditional "prejudices" are too deeply and habitually inscribed to remove merely by noting them. Thus to shorten the process the phenomenologist may resort to a certain heideggerian "violence" with words. This "violence" I undertake purposefully and use Parmenides as my mentor in the practice. At first my descriptions will seem metaphorical, literary instead of the usual literal-minded "philosophy" we are used to.

I would note that this use of language arises out of phenomenology itself as it seeks to unlayer and upset traditions. Students of phenomenology invariably find that upon first turning to experience words seem to fail them and a struggle with language begins which first issues forth in apparent metaphors and neologisms. This use of language stands at the opposite pole of a continuum which has as its other extreme a certain hardening of language into a schematicism which congeals and sometimes no longer "reveals." My aim here is to remain short of congealment, but at the same time to suggest something stronger than metaphor. I therefore ask that you allow me to "play" with words. This "play" is deliberately suggestive. It elicits rather than deduces. In this sense "poetry" is not accidental to phenomenology, but essential.

At the same time this suggestiveness is directed. It calls for you to observe your own experiences and note their characteristics. Of course I cannot expect anyone to confirm or deny everything I note without having undertaken sufficiently the observations and variations called for. I will thus find myself caught between what appears as a temporary "dogmatism" of description on one side and, in an attempt to use ordinary rather than unusual examples, an easily misunderstood "common sense" interpretation on the other. Between these extremes I wish to intrude the epoché and its heideggerian poetic "violence" which is meant only to remove or suspend assumptions and never to reduce the fullness of experience.

(C) Examples are arrived at in the use of free variations which have as their aim the pointing up of essential characteristics, structures, invariants. This intuition through examples, *Wesenschau*, I greatly reduce here to a few paradigm cases. I shall, for the most part, use only easily understandable ones.

(D) I wish to presuppose, in addition to the general reduction above, two sets of concepts used phenomenologically. (1) I wish to distinguish between *field* characteristics and *entity* characteristics. In a rough sense this is the difference between "whole" and "part" but it also relates in a rough sense to a heideggerian Being and being's distinction. In the description to follow Sound refers to the field and sounds to the sound-entities of the field. (2) I shall assume the usual descriptive characteristics of consciousness which I here term the *core* (for the focus of attention), *fringe* (for the marginal or implicit aspects of consciousness), and *horizon* (for the limit of boundary of consciousness).

(E) And, finally, I would like to employ an extraphenomenological device—at some risk. That extraphenomenological device is the beginning use of the ordinary notions of a division into five senses and of a difference between space and time. I am well aware that these distinctions may get in the way of what I ultimately want to show. Clearly, for example, experience in its most concrete form is global and not neatly divided into five discrete senses. At best one may *focus* upon a sense— but the other senses are present in the margins and never absent. Thus confusions may easily enter. Clearly, also from the phenomenological perspective, "lived" time is not separate from its spatiality. I take the risks of using these distinctions as heuristic devices only because they short-cut the more tedious or too "violent" route into a description too easily full of a phenomenological "tribal language."

A PHENOMENOLOGY OF AUDITORY EXPERIENCE

The Shape of Sound is Round.

Sound comes in two primary spatial dimensions. Sound is directional and sound is encompassing. And, at first curiously, neither dimension is lacking in any given experience of sound, although one of these dimensions may "stand out" in relative prominence over the other depending upon the situation and the intention in the situation.

First, directionality: In our ordinary course of affairs we are quite aware of sounds which appear directionally. If the automobile horn honks behind me I quickly jump out of its way. I hear the sound of the typewriter down the hall. There are my two colleagues arguing again and they are in David's office this time instead of Ed's. In fact, expanded examples rightly amaze us with the clarity and distinctness possible in relation to directionality. Georg von Békésy in his studies upon localization cites the fact that the building of straight roads in eastern European forests depended upon just this ability. One man would stand on one side of the woods and yell loudly and the second would proceed straight towards him marking trees on the way thus creating a straight path. And in WW I, aircraft location, in a day when sounds were more clearly sounds *of* the aircraft, was accomplished by means of two extended trumpets set into the ears to locate the direction of the aircraft before its visual spotting. A variation of this same technique has been used by the Vietnamese in recent years. By standing at the bottom of a bomb crater, an "unnatural" natural receiving bowl, the guerilla is able to detect the direction of coming planes minutes before they are spotted and thus warn his company of their approach. In many aspects of ordinary affairs we focus upon sounds as directional.

But the encompassing characteristics of sound are never absent, even if placed on the fringe by our attending consciousness. The ticking of the clock, though coming from the dresser, also surrounds me. By merely shifting the focus of my attention I can note, within limits in this case, the dimension of encompassing which the ticking displays.

At the opposite end of the continuum where the encompassing characteristics of sound are most clearly present stands the example of listening to music. Well built stereos and well built auditoria are designed so as to maximize an immersion in sound. I am surrounded by the symphony which at an optimal peak is so total that I find it difficult to tell whether it is "in the middle of my head" or "out there"—the usual inner and outer distinctions become blurred. It is in this phenomenon that the round shape of sound is first suggested and the hoary head of Parmenides lurks below us.

But I must now allow a resurrection too soon lest his spectre frighten us from seeing other relevant aspects of the phenomenon before us. If sound is both dimensional and encompassing and if one characteristic seems to stand out in certain experiences and the other in different experiences we have yet no basis for relating these differences to consciousness in its structural characteristics.

Between the optimal immersion in music and the concentric focus upon direction stand a whole series of auditory phenomena. Attend for a moment to a catalogue of auditory occasions within a given duration of consciousness. Given, all at once, are a plethora of *sounds*. The furnace is roaring; the clock is ticking; the page of my wife's book is flicking; the dog is barking; the traffic on the road is humming; the birds are singing; etc. Here I note three things. First, all of these things are going on at the same time but I have great trouble paying attention equally to them at the same time. Indeed, as I catalogue I find the focus of my attention switches subtly from one to another. But at the same time the other sounds are noticeably present on the fringes of my awareness. Second, I note that this catalogue is of *sounds*, entities with which my field is filled, atoms as it were, of sound. Third, insofar as these sounds appear directionally they are on a common sense level all "sounds of _____," *i.e.*, the auditory expressions of entities. Directionality appears as essentially connected to sounds.

Now a new question poses itself—can I note any field characteristics of Sound? And, if this is possible, what are the characteristics of the auditory field strictly as a field? The observation itself seems very difficult to make. It runs counter to my usual habits of attention. Usually I am focused upon this or that entity; I am concerned with this or that thing. In heideggerian language, I am "forgetful" of the ground of things, of the Being of beings.

At first my attempts are crude and additive, I attempt to *construct* the field of sound. The sound of the clock is to the right; the sound of the dog is slightly behind; the traffic to the left; etc. By this crude process of addition and perhaps by making inferences I light upon the possibility that one field characteristic of Sound is its "roundness"—the field of Sound encompasses me. This structure of the auditory field, however, need not be arrived at in this indirect way because it is also "given at a stroke" as Merleau-Ponty might say and we have already noted it in the paradigm example of sound in its encompassing dimension. The experience of music accomplished this "immediately." If you will understand me carefully and remain within the husserlian notion in which examples, even a single example, may give an intuition of an essence, then I might well say that music is a privileged instance in which field characteristics of Sound are revealed.

One such characteristic of the field of Sound is its encompassing of me, of my consciousness. But there are other field characteristics as well. Sound is a plenum, always full even if that fullness displays different textures and intensifies. So long as I am conscious (and am not stone deaf) Sound is present. Sound is, in this sense, continuous as well. Even in the desert and in an echo chamber there are still small sounds. In terms of the field of Sound, "I" am the centre around which the constant field of Sound extends indefinitely as a "roundness." The shape of Sound is round and I am in the middle. Parmenides rises. But is "round" too strong? Is it merely metaphorical? Because if it is round it must have a boundary, a horizon, no matter how indefinite and hard to locate. Where does Sound "end"? What is the horizon of Sound?

The Horizon of Sound Is Silence

As soon as the question of a horizon of Sound is raised the limitations upon the ordinary uses of space and time also come into view. As I move towards "time" in its phenomenological sense in auditory experience the "spatiality" of Sound begins to take on a certain strangeness for common sense. A certain heideggerian making-strange-of-the-familiar begins to intrude. I make this approximation by introducing the thesis that *silence* is the horizon of Sound.

I begin with sounds, the entity terms of auditory experience. What happens with a sound? In the parmenidean sense, appearances "come into being and pass from being." This is clearly the case with sounds. "BOOM"—the explosion startles as it suddenly appears and almost as suddenly disappears. More gently, the sound of the train comes from nothing, gradually slipping into consciousness and when down the track in the other direction gradually fades out of presence. It comes from "nothing" and disappears into "nothing." What is the "nothing"? The "nothing" is *silence*, the horizon of sound is silence. There is a boundary which at the edge of sound passes over into non-experience.

Take the case of the "top" and "bottom" of the ability to hear sounds. If we momentarily import the universe of discourse used by the acoustician, we are able to hear sounds "up to" a certain frequency and "down to" a certain frequency beyond which they pass into—silence. The same boundary phenomenon occurs with volume. A horizon is reached at the low end of the scale such that a barely discernible sound finally disappears—into silence. And, in the days of hard rock music, a certain loudness at the edge of our hearing ability where sound gives way to pain brings a certain "silence" in which sounds "disappear." Before and after a discrete sound's existence there is "silence" and all gesturing towards the boundaries are gestures towards silence.

But we are dealing here with sounds as entity terms for which silence is clearly relative, relative to the particular sounds. This is the parmenidean "coming into being and passing from being" which applies to entities and not to the field as field. Sounds are the inconstants which occur against the background of Sound as the constant field of conscious experience. But nevertheless, one reaches a boundary here, too. In every direction I find a horizon to the sphere of Sound, the horizon is "all around." That horizon is the "edge" which passes ever into silence. But silence is not a presence. In fact, silence is not given, but is a limit concept. Silence as the horizon of Sound is never given, but is reached. It may be noted, but not named in the parmenidean sense, for, when reached it is the way of not-being which the goddess noted for Parmenides as the limit. "That it is not and that not-being must be, cannot be grasped by my mind; for you cannot know not-being and cannot express it."[1] Silence is inexpressible; it is not-being. It is the horizon which "surrounds" Sound. But I am no longer sure that the "all around" is spatial in the ordinary sense at all. It is rather my "lived space" which is "surrounded" by the horizon of silence.

The Sound of Silence is Time.

I have so far spoken of some apparent "spatial" characteristics of Sound as encompassing, continuously present, and at its borders "surrounded" by a horizon of silence. What happens if we change our focus to the temporal characteristics of Sound? Do the same characteristics show themselves?

I have noted how, within the field of consciousness, sounds "come into being" and "pass from being"—but under the category of temporality something more radical seems to happen. I will illustrate this by turning to one set of phenomenological experiments which reveal what I shall call an *echo-phenomenon*, the significance of which I shall only suggest here.

I return to the paradigm case of listening to music to illustrate the temporal characteristics of sounds and Sound. It was clear that within the field of consciousness distinct sounds appear and disappear, but that the field is never empty as such. This is also the case with a single piece of music. Separate notes may come into being and pass from being although the piece as a whole continues to sound. But, temporally speaking, it also may be said that the piece as a whole continues to

---

1. Philip Wheelwright (editor), *The Presocratics*, New York: The Odyssey Press, Inc., 1966, p. 96.

sound. But, temporally speaking, it also may be said that the piece as it is being presented comes into being and passes from being in a conscious duration. As a present it begins, it arrives with a "temporal edge" which trails off into another "fading edge" as it passes with the stream of consciousness into the past. And in the ordinary attitude we must say that the piece is passing through its current temporal embodiment. But this way of posing the question already pre-supposes a loaded objectivist "metaphysic" which presumes the constancies of "real" entities somewhere "outside" experience. That this judgment may be made, I do not question; it is, after all, just one aspect of what Husserl called the "natural attitude." But our task is to note the phenomenological, concrete aspects of the phenomenon apart from such judgments.

It is not accidental, in my opinion, that Husserl in his *Phenomenology of Inner Time Consciousness* turned to music for his primary example. My experiments were first made within the context of checking out the claims made by Husserl concerning protention, retention, and recollection as well as comparing these descriptions with the modifications made by Merleau-Ponty and their transformation into extases by Heidegger. Briefly and simply put, the general phenomenological characteristics of the temporal field should show that (a) there is no "point" or instant of time consciousness. An instant is as much an abstraction as a pure quale and is part of the metaphysical machinery of sense-data atomism and not an experiential given. Rather, there is a "span" or duration of consciousness within which a multiplicity of occurrences are present and which are related in terms of before and after. I would note, in passing, that several ambiguities regarding the use of the word "present" get involved here. In the broad sense of "present" which I shall term the parmenidean sense, even the future and past are "present" insofar as they are concretely intended. But there is a second sense of "present" as that which is immediately or concretely being made present. The process of making-present or becoming present, however, may be described. Finally there is the conceptually present as an ideal point, the instant which is conceived, not lived. Phenomenology, in its implicit metaphysic, re-arranges the ordering of these meanings.

(b) At the "leading edge" of the temporal field Husserl locates a protention, a future-directed anticipation which in the case of music is realized in the expectation-intention which focuses upon the next possibilities of the melody, for example. This feature of consciousness is extremely functionally important for the modern jazz musician who plays with his peers by knowing the right notes to play in relation to the direction the musical "language" is taking. His part in the "dialogue" is based upon an intuitive awareness of the living jazz "language." This may be contrasted, at least in part, with the traditional musician who "translates" or "reads" a language already given in the notation which assures that the piece "speaks" the same "language."

(c) At the "trailing" or "after-edge" of temporal consciousness lies *retention*, the process of "fading off" into the past as we ordinarily might say. Retention is the still-present reverberation of the sound which has come into being and which is in the process of passing out of being. It is still vivid, but is already being superseded by the next movement of the music.

(d) And, finally, it is also important for us to note that retention as a fading out of consciousness is different from *recollection* which, in ordinary terms is a bringing back, a representing of a past phenomenon. A re-called entity is made present as having occurred, but as not now (perceptually) present. To pass from a phenomenology of inner time consciousness with its "trailing edge" of retention to recollection is also to pass from a phenomenology of time to a phenomenology of memory. And memory with its recollections is a species of imaginatively represented entities.

Now my experiment: I was listening to a Vivaldi piece on my stereo. I first focussed upon the question of duration and, in short, found the husserlian claims for the most part well founded. I could never find an instant of perceived sound, but always found only a duration which had "leading" and "trailing" edges within which a multiplicity of things occurred. I then began to attempt "stretching" this duration to locate its fringes and horizon. I posed myself the question—how "much" is "contained" in this duration and where does it "end"? This, as I expected on the basis of the same problems in the "spatial" category, turned out to be extremely difficult. That is, to note fringe and horizon characteristics is very hard precisely because consciousness is ordinarily focused *within* the whole. Horizons and fringes, moreover, are always vague rather than sharp and distinct. And this clearly was the case with the temporal horizon as well. Yet it did appear that my protending consciousness could locate a "welling up" into presence of sounds from the silence of the future. It was also the case that I did have expectations in relation to the musical context being presented. In the case of Vivaldi these expectations were fairly concrete and clear—I should have been greatly confused and surprised if he had suddenly shifted his musical "language." Instead the music easily "funnelled" into the proper "language." (As interesting variations note the confusion one gets in first listening to a new musical "language." At first it is even difficult to recognize it as music, then later, even if its musicality is granted, one's expectations are confused and a much greater amount of concentration must go into listening, very like the great efforts that have to be made to understand a new tongue one is learning.)

But even so, I am not an accomplished musician so my expectations are still relatively uninformed. It was in the context of "stretching" in the other direction that the echo-phenomenon occurred. I again found the observation difficult. I tried to focus upon the fading away of sounds into the past and see how "long" they remained present and how they "faded off." Normally our temporal focus tends to be "toward" the peak of that which is being-presented in contrast to the fringe awareness of "fading-off." Nevertheless I could note the reverberations of the notes being played as they "faded off" and I tried to keep them retained as long as possible. But I found myself getting them back in an echo-like effect. The "just-past" sounds began to recur, overlapped with the perceptually presented sounds. Until suddenly, I received what I shall call a fully "doubled passage."

For the sake of simplicity allow me to use a hypothetical example to illustrate the experience. Let us say that a passage of six notes occurs in which three are found within my perception of the now-melody with one or two more fading off. In the echo-phenomenon of a "double-passage" the three just past re-appeared as vividly and as fully as the now-melody of the three notes now playing. That is, I "heard" two sets of chords playing at the same time. It was as if someone had just dropped the needle upon a second record player at a point on the record just a part of a second later than the point of the record which had originally been playing.

I was startled—but since that time I have been able to repeat the phenomenon from time to time although I find a much fainter version of it quite easy to do, in which case it is clearly an "echo-phenomenon" within auditory experience. Thus to the click-clack of the washing machine I may imaginatively add the re-collected "click-clack" of the just faded sound in such a way that both the perceived sound and the recalled sounds are present with one the echo of the other.

The extreme case of the phenomenon in which the perceived retention and the recollected presentation formed a complete synthesis is of great interest to me because of its related possibilities. For example, it is well known that schizophrenics are prone to auditory, in contrast to visual, hallucinations. They hear voices—and in some cases, it is reported, the voice they hear is strangely like their own. I have noted elsewhere that one form of thinking is an "inner speech" which I believe to be an auditory imagination, but an auditory imagination which is so familiar or close to us that it is hard to note and mostly taken for granted. I believe my now controllable auditory "double sound" is related to both these phenomena. (The doubled music in this case, however, is a creature of extreme concentration, structurally more akin to the experience of the mystics than to the evidently uncontrollable "voices" of the schizophrenic.) The unified "double sound" synthesizes what is often a set of distinguishable activities. Note a continuum from separation to synthesis in the following examples: I am driving a car and attending to the traffic, the road, etc. But at the same time I am thinking of my income tax forms which I must fill out this week and wondering how much I can get back from the government. My broadly conceived "imaginative" activity is distinct from the bodily-perceptual activity which, although not at all absent from awareness, seems almost "automatic." Closer to an example of concentration is the case of looking at a pretty girl and at the same time thinking intensely of that pretty girl. Finally, one reaches one extreme moment of concentration in the moment when one is fully aware seemingly *only* of the object within consciousness. In phenomenological language the core of attention is thoroughly and intensely concentrated upon a single phenomenon.

But my example is also different from this continuum in that something was "added to" the perceived phenomenon. If the husserlian distinctions hold, the doubling was one in which retention was doubled with recollection to form the auditory illusion.

It is at this point that I return, once again, to Parmenides and resurrect a parmenidean hypothesis. Does temporality, like spatiality, in reference to auditory experience have a horizon of silence? Is it, too, a well-bounded plenum? It seems that this is the case, for in "stretching" one's attention to the extreme fringe of the "trailing edge" of time consciousness one reaches a point beyond which it is difficult, if not impossible to go. A more concentrated effort only succeeds in breaking the effort with the rebound of an echo. The temporal field is a constant in Parmenidean terms, but it is reached not without, but *with* the extremest evidence of the senses. Thus "time" in its parmenidean sense is *within* the present in its broadest sense rather than the present being in time. Furthermore, the horizon of temporality is the silence of future and past which never *are* unless "made present" in concrete form. Silence is the horizon which is reached but never given. But silence is the enigma of both time and space, the well bounded limit of auditory experience.

The Sphere of Sound.

My summary of Sound re-sounds Parmendes. For the experience of Sound reaches its horizon within which its being is that of a well-filled plenum. Its boundaries are either spatial or temporal, if indeed, such distinctions make sense at all. Of Being *and* of the *field* of consciousness (as field) one can say with Parmenides: "It is, whole, still, and without end . . . it simply is or it simply is not."[2] All this is descriptive when said of the field of consciousness as field.

But at the end we are unsatisfied. Is Parmenides' word the ultimate or the penultimate word? I pose three questions: (1) Who is the being who recognized the horizon of his conscious being so that, in recognizing it, he transcends it? Parmenides, unlike phenomenology, does not raise the question of the questioner. Nor does he describe intentionality. Instead he says, "thinking and the object of thought are the same"[3] but surely this is an enigmatic saying. It is one thing to say the knower is essentially related to the known, but another to say the knower is the known. To leave the matter with Parmenides is to invite idealism. (2) What of the internal "music" of the sphere? In the end what Parmenides says applies only to the field of consciousness as a field so far as the way of Being is said. But everything of human interest is within the field, a matter of appearances, of the way of opinion in which there is coming to be and passing from being. Sound "contains" sounds, but sounds are the music of the sphere. (3) And, finally, is there some sense in which everything comes from Nothing? Does sound come from Silence? In short, does anything new come-to-be? That if it comes to be it must come to be within the sphere of consciousness must be the case, but does transcendence makes its most significant aim an aim at the unsayable of Parmenides? What comes from the Silence of the Future?

---

2. *Ibid.*, p. 97.
3. *Ibid.*, p. 98.

CHAPTER SEVEN

Parmenidean Puzzles

Central to Parmenides' philosophy are the distinctions between ways of thinking. Two such distinctions, recognized from antiquity, are the *way of truth* which is necessary and the *way of seeming* which is relative. Commentators, at least since Simplicius, have held that parallel to these distinctions are those between reason and perception.

> Parmenides effects the transition from objects of reason to objects of sense, or as he himself puts it, from truth to seeming, when he writes, "Here I end my trustworthy discourse and thought concerning truth; henceforth learn the beliefs of mortal men..."[1]

I shall argue that *as Parmenides puts it*, the transition from the way of truth to the way of seeming is *not* a transition from reason to perception. Rather, the reason for the relativity of the way of seeming arises from the process Parmenides calls *naming* which is in effect the positing of entities.

To my knowledge only one ancient commentator clearly recognizes the close association of reason and perception. Theophrastus indicates, "For Parmenides regards perception and thought as the same."[2]

I shall argue that for Parmenides a formula, *being equals thought equals perception,* can account for the way of truth—if perception is taken in a certain way. The same equation, taking perception in another

---

1. G. S. Kirk and J. E. Raven, *The Presocaratic Philosophers* (Cambridge: The Cambridge University Press, 1964), p. 278.
2. *Ibid.*, p. 282.

way, through the process of positing entities, can account for the way of seeming.

This argument arises out of insights which stem from Heidegger's discussion of the pre-Socratics.

Basic to Heidegger's philosophy is the distinction between being (*Sein*) and beings (*Seiendes*) which functionally is that between whole and parts. Being is the whole, the unity which underlies all entities or things. According to Heidegger, Pre-Socratic philosophy consists of the gradual uncovering of things or entities out of the whole of being. This discovery of the Greeks is paralleled by a gradual shift of interest in the whole to an interest in things as such.[3] For Heidegger, Parmenides stands at the very beginning of the philosophical uncovering of the origin of things out of the whole of being.

My adaptation of Heidegger's being/beings distinction consists of an association of whole/parts in relation to perception. The further suggestion that Parmenides isolates the way in which entities arise is adapted in the second part of the argument which shows how the way of seeming is dependent upon the naming of positing of entities.

The second insight offered by Heidegger and presupposed here is that Parmenides distinguishes between three rather than two paths of thought. The first path is the way of truth or the way of being which must be thought. The way of truth is necessary. There is a second way, the way of non-being, which may be noted but which *cannot* be thought. The way of non-being is the contradictory of the way of being. The goddess of the Proem merely wishes Parmenides to note this negative way. The *third* way, however, is the way of seeming. It arises, as we shall see, by combining the first two ways. It is with the third way that things emerge and that names are given.

The stage is now set for the two arguments I wish to elaborate: (1) The Formula, being equals thought equals perception, can make sense of the many "odd" things Parmenides actually says of being. (2) The distinction between the way of truth and the way of seeming does not depend upon a distinction between thought and perception, but upon the process of naming which functions as a convention regarding entities.

* * *

3. This point is repeatedly made by Heidegger in his *Introduction to Metaphysics* (Garden City: Doubleday and Co., 1961).

(1) Being equals thought equals perception accounts for the description of being within the way of truth. If one applies common sense criteria to the statements of Parmenides concerning being, the result is bound to be a recognition of "oddity." This is particularly the case when it is recalled that Parmenides considered these statements to be necessary. Being must be thought and said in just this way.

The statements are as follows: (I begin in reverse order so that the "oddity" is emphasized.) (a) Being is like a well-rounded sphere. (b) Being is full, immovable, describable by terms such as continuous, complete, whole, and homogeneous. (c) Being is simply now, without beginning or end, without coming into being or passing from it.

Now as I move to a description of how perception, taken in a certain way, can account for such "odd" statements, note the advice of Parmenides, "Gaze steadfastly at things, which though far away, are yet present to the mind. For you cannot cut off being from being; it does not scatter itself into a universe and then reunify."[4] Here one is cautioned not to break up the sphere of being, for it is *this* which leads to confusion. What leads to confusion is *not* perception as such, but the following of custom. "Do not let custom, born of everyday experience, tempt your eyes to be aimless, your ear and tongue to be echoes."[5]

Parmenides does not tell us to abandon our eyes and ears at all, but to abandon our ordinary assumptions regarding things. He asks us to abandon "all the usual notions that mortals accept and rely on as if true—coming-to-be and perishing, being and not-being, change of place and variegated shades of color—these are nothing more than names."[6] If we follow Parmenides and "bracket out" all the assumptions we make about things and at the same time gaze steadfastly, how can we justify the statements made concerning being?

I shall use the visual field as a paradigm case, but I suspect other senses would serve as well. Now if I were to ask you now, "What do you see?" I suspect the answer would ordinarily be something like "I see people, chairs, a lectern, etc." But this will not do, for we have been asked specifically to abandon all ordinary assumptions about *things* which move, come into being and perish, etc. Rather we must take the visual field in only a certain way.

---

4. Philip Wheelwright (ed.), *The Presocratics* (New York: The Odyssey Press, 1966), p. 96.
5. *Ibid.*, p. 96.
6. *Ibid.*, p. 98.

We must take the visual field *strictly as a whole*. And negatively we must make no judgments concerning sensory "objects" which fill the field. Again, if I were to go to a blackboard and draw an "X" and ask what one sees, the ordinary response would be "I see an X." But of course we literally see more than this. As any good gestaltist or phenomenologist would be quick to point out we actually see "X"—on blackboard—in room—etc. The "X" that we say we see has been selected out of the entire visual field as an object of attention. Note also that the clues which surround the first question regarding "what do you see?" also serve to establish a convention by which we make the ordinary response.

But we can, in the phenomenologists' sense, also direct our attention to the visual field as a whole. Now note what description must follow if the visual field is so taken. (a) Taken strictly as a whole the visual field appears as—*a well-rounded sphere*. Parmenides says that being is a well-rounded sphere; truth is well rounded; and now in our illustration the visual field is also well rounded.

Now I grant that this may seem "odd," but it is odd in a quite different sense from the "oddity" with which we began. Perhaps the *taking* of visual field in this way remains "odd" in relation to common sense; but within its new context, the "being" of the visual field as a well-rounded sphere is no longer odd, but is rather a necessary way to accurately describe the field as a whole.

But is this correlation between being-thought-perception more than a mere coincidence? Further corroboration must be sought in the descriptions Parmenides gives concerning the well-rounded sphere of being. (b) Recall that it is also full, continuous, and whole. Again, the visual field taken strictly as a whole is full, continuous, and whole. Within the visual field there are no breaks at all. For example, if one considers the visual field solely as a color field, it becomes immediately obvious that nowhere within the field as a whole is there a lack of color. We would certainly be surprised were we suddenly to find a colorless gap in our visual field! Further, the visual field is constantly full and whole—there are no gaps of "non-being." Being-thought-perception is full, continuous, and whole.

The sphere of being is also immovable. At first glance this may seem harder to establish—but after some thought and by sticking strictly to our paradigm of the visual field as a whole, the immobility of being may be seen. For motion to occur there must be more than one entity. Either motion occurs relatively between two or more entities, or it occurs in relation to some ideal standard, an ideal entity. With the single sphere of being, however, no motion can occur, for there is nothing by which movement could be judged. This holds for the visual field as well. We have but a single visual field and there is no other appearance by which to judge any motion of the sphere as a whole.

Here objections might be raised: is there not motion *within* the visual field? The answer to this is at first simple, for as soon as one speaks of motion within the whole, one is no longer regarding the field as a whole. Nor is this answer a mere quibble. For the very basis by which one may establish motion within the whole presupposes the breaking up of that whole into parts which is the establishing of entities. This will be important for the second part of my argument.

We have now being-thought-perception as a well-rounded sphere which is full, continuous, whole and immovable. (c) Parmenides says that it is simply *now*, without beginning or end, without coming into being or passing from it. This description is a bit more difficult to deal with, but the parallel between being and the visual field remains. The visual field does appear as simply now—it is there. Moreover we do not see it come into being or pass from being. It is more than merely interesting to note that Parmenides asks in this regard, "How could you go about investigating its birth?"[7] If it were not the case that being always simply is now, where could you go to get evidence of its being otherwise? For whenever we gaze on the whole of being, it is simply there.

Here an objection might arise: what happens with being as visual when we close our eyes and then open them again? Though I am not completely satisfied with my own answers, I would at least argue that: (i) Parmenides may have merely taken being as real. Being, or for that matter the visual field, does not depend upon the subject; (ii) in the second part of my argument, I shall attempt to show that all relativities depend upon the positing of entities. To say that being disappears when we close our eyes and comes into being when we open them is to have already posited two entities—being and myself as subject. (iii) And Finally, I am now thoroughly convinced that something quite different actually happens when we close our eyes. The visual field does not in fact disappear; it merely turns dark. I would even hazard saying that it retains its well-

---

7. *Ibid.*, p. 97.

rounded characteristic, though this may be harder to distinguish under such conditions. Being-thought-perception always is simply now.

The visual field, taken strictly as a whole, is a well-rounded sphere, full, continuous, immovable, simply present now. Being equals thought equals perception.

(2) I shall now retrace the argument with a different end in mind, to clarify the way of seeming as the way which arises when entities are posited through the process of naming. The way of truth, of being, of the whole, was considered necessary by Parmenides. But he did not stop with the description of the way of truth. Rather he went on to say at least as much about the way of seeming.

In the Proem, the rationale for following out both the way of truth and the way of seeming is outlined: "It is needful that you learn of all matters—both the unshaken heart of well-rounded truth and the opinion of mortals which lack true belief."[8] A purpose is assigned to this full investigation of both truth and seeming, "For it is useful that by passing everything under review you should learn this also—how to judge mere seeming."[9] Parmenides wished to judge the way of seeming, the relative way.

What is the source of this way of seeming in which necessary truth is replaced by relativity? The answer Parmenides gives can best be seen, I would hold, if one accepts Heidegger's notion of three ways. I have already described the way of being; the second way, the way of non-being, cannot be described, it cannot be thought, nor can it be perceived—though it can be noted. The third way, the way of seeming, arises by combining the first two ways in the separation of entities out from the whole of being.

The way of seeming is always described in terms of sets of pairs by Parmenides.

> I warn you against another path, along which mortals wander ignorantly, with divided minds and scattered thoughts, so befuddled and helpless as to resemble the blind and deaf. There are crowds of them. without discernment, maintaining that [note the pairs now to come] to be and not to be are the same and not the same, and that everything is in a state of movement and counter movement.[10]

---

8. *Ibid.*, p. 96.
9. *Ibid.*, p. 97.
10. *Ibid.*, p. 97.

It is this pairing which lies at the basis of custom, born of everyday experience, which leads one's eyes, ears, and tongue astray. And at the very basis of all the pairs found in the way of seeming lies the separation out from the whole of being of entities. Once this occurs error can enter and uncertainty is bound to result due to the many possible ways to arrange entities.

This separation of entities out of the whole sphere of being is what Parmenides calls naming. With naming things arise "Thus according to common opinion things came into being, thus they are now, and they at length after they have reached maturity they will perish. To each kind of thing men have assigned a distinctive name."[11]

Such named entities are listed in terms of three sets of pairs by Parmenides: (a) coming to be and perishing; (b) being and not-being; and (c) change of place and variegated shades of color. These, says Parmenides, are nothing more than names.

I now return to the paradigm case of the visual field, now taken as broken up into entities, and describe the way of seeming. If one assumes that the visual field is made up of entities, various results follow. Consider the visual field abstractly as a color field. As a whole it is totally colored—but it also contains "colors." But note what happens in this distinction of whole to parts. By recognizing colors, we also "break up" the whole and posit entities. By the very movement by which we distinguish colors from color, we also posit entity in relation to whole.

It turns out that each of Parmenides' pairs in the way of seeming can be illustrated in relation to the visual field as modified by taking it as a collection of entities. The last pair is the most difficult. (c) Change of place and variegated shades of color is a pair which is a mere name or custom.

It is quite clear with this pair that change of place does make sense only if one has already posited entities. Only if the whole of being is made up of entities can there be change of place. For so long as the whole is considered strictly, there can be no change of place. But note that change of place is paired by Parmenides with variegated color. Could it be that Parmenides is linking the rise of entities with an association of color change?

Imagine the visual sphere to be entirely gray—were it so it is clear that entities could not be posited. But within the whole "colors" appear and

---

11. *Ibid.*, p. 100.

these appearances can be divided up and associated with entities and hence change of place can occur. Imagine a small world, already "entitized" in which there is a flat white backdrop in front of which there stands a black pole and between the white backdrop and black pole there swings an orange circle on a pendulum. As the orange circle swings back and forth it passes between the black pole and the white backdrop. Now of course I have used "entity language" to describe the scene. In this case we could say that the orange circle as it passed behind the black pole changed place—but we could also say that its "place" was associated with a change of color because all that appears to us at the time it is behind the pole is black pole against white backdrop. Expand this illustration and I suspect a key to Parmenides' pairing of change of place with change of color is located.

The other two pairs are much easier to handle in relation to the basic process of naming entities. (a) The pair of coming-into-being and perishing necessarily presupposes the positing of entities within the visual field as a whole. If one considers a flower (entity) as it grows and dies, and if one attributes identity to that flower, then it may be said to appear as coming-into-being and perishing. But it is necessary to first posit it as an entity. For if one returns to the way of necessary truth concerning the whole, again as a visual field, one must say that so far as the field as a whole is concerned, it is just as full after the flower has perished as before. Only appearances have changed—but appearances are already entities.

The second pair (b) of being and not-being parallel the above case. Only entities can be *and* not-be. A puff of smoke "is" at the moment and "is not" at the next. But again, strictly speaking, the visual field as a whole is no less full after the smoke disappears than before.

In each case it may now be seen that the relation between the way of being and the way of seeming depends upon how the visual sphere is taken. In the first case it is taken strictly as a whole; in the second it is "broken up" into entities and entities are focused upon. It is this latter process that Parmenides described as the opinion of ordinary mortals and this is the process of naming or establishing custom. This naming or entitizing of the whole, however useful for everyday concerns, cannot carry with it necessity. One can always make errors concerning entities. Errors occur only in relation to entities.

The question may now arise: is not the breaking up of the sphere of being itself necessary? Is not naming necessary? The answer is, of course, yes, but in the sense that it is necessary for everyday experience and not for pure contemplation as such. Recall, after all, that *Parmenides did* say just as much about the way of seeming as he did about the way of truth. The philosophic question, however, is one of priority. One must know the way of truth in order to *judge* the way of seeming.

I may now summarize my argument: I have attempted to show that the division between the way of truth and the way of seeming in no way need be paralleled by a division between reason and perception. Rather, the distinction depends upon how perception is taken. In the way of truth, it is taken strictly as a whole and what is there seen is necessary. In the way of seeming, dependent upon the custom of naming, the separation out of the whole of entities, what is seen must always be considered relative. The way of truth must stand as the standard for the way of seeming—but both retain the relation of perception to thought.

CHAPTER EIGHT

Sense and Sensuality

Were you to look at the best sellers' list this week you would find at least three or four of the leading non-fiction books dealing with sex. In the fiction category sex is so pervasive that to find a book without at least one vivid scene of coupling would be a considerable task. But between the non-fiction and the fiction books there exists a gap. The non-fiction entries seem to be dominated by a "technology of sex": techniques, physiology (or "plumbing"), all described in clinical terms as if some observant Martian were viewing us as a curious race of "interesting mating animals" with an insatiable passion for copulation.

In the fiction category there is a certain detachment as well—but with a different emphasis. The copulators in this category are mainly self-enclosed subjects rich only in fantasy life. Indeed, one such book consists of the recitation of the wandering thoughts, daydreams and memories of a woman undergoing seven minutes of intercourse.

It occurred to me that this plethora of often asexual books about sex did indeed say something about our post-Victorian preoccuptation. The pattern seems to be that either we regard sexuality as the mechanical action of an object-like body which needs to be tuned up now and then to perform well, or we regard sexual relations as the excuse for subjective fantasies. In short, the glut of literature can be seen as a form of *institutionalized cartesianism*. We are acting out the dictums concerning man as body-machine whose interior, private self is inhabited by "mental events," the vestigial remains of the cartesian thinking substance. And we are troubled by the connections, usually vague associations, between ourselves as objectified bodies and our hermetically sealed inner experience.

A very serious instance of the contemporary tendency to take cartesianism literally exists in a mental state, schizoid in form, called "depersonalization" by J. M. Heaton:

> In depersonalization the patient feels compelled to observe his own actions like a spectator. This has a destructive effect on the immediacy of his experience and almost any area of it may be affected. Thus every thought and emotion may be taken to bits and the patient may feel like an automaton without a will of his own.
>
> His spatial experience may be altered so that the world seems perfectly still, like a postcard. Things may seem remote and often there is a general impression of flatness. Time is altered so that there is no longer a sense of becoming and all seems timeless, unchanging and hopeless.
>
> The patient's experience of his body is often changed so that it may feel strange and as if it was not his own; often the patient feels he is existing mainly in his own head, usually somewhere behind his eyes through which he has to peer out. ("Depersonalization and the Development of Visual Literacy," J. M. Heaton, *Confinia Psychiatrica*, 11, 1968, p. 181.)

This experience is cartesian even to the final location of the observer consciousness somewhere in the head behind the eyes—perhaps in the pituitary gland thought to be the connecting place between the body and the soul.

I could be tempted at this point to begin an extended and direct attack upon this version of cartesianism and its inadequacies, particularly in regard to experience—but instead I shall merely note it as a background problem which pervades our beliefs and language. Instead of an attack, I want to begin a retracing of a path back towards a careful examination of the richness and complexity of concrete experience and this in the context of a phenomenology of eros. Even in the realm of the erotic the cartesian dissociation of me from my body and from my acts has occurred.

My strategy will be one taken by phenomenological and existential philosophers. I wish to affirm that *I am my body*—but that this embodiment which I am and which I enact is not that of cartesian machine, but of a person of living flesh. After a brief comment about such a phenomenology I wish to outline (a) some characteristics of the experience of *touch* as they relate to structural features of experience; (b) then move the discussion to some of our rites of invitation which encircle our "lived space" and which relate to sexual spatial constitution; and (c) finally, I shall indicate why, from the preceding considerations, the sexual act even in relation to touch and distance is privileged in certain respects.

Phenomenology at its inception began both as an anti-cartesian polemic and as an attempt to recover the clues for a full appreciation of experience. Husserl, particularly in the *Crisis*, began to speak of a *lifeworld* and of the embodied person, and certainly the existential phenomenologies have continued to investigate the implications of this recovery of experience, particularly Gabriel Marcel and Maurice Merleau-Ponty. In this philosophical attempt to recover the full sense of what it means to be a creature of flesh the central feature of experience was termed *intentionality*. This term, as used by phenomenologists, characterizes the structural features of experience (also called subjectivity or consciousness).

In briefest form intentionality unites sensing and signification, perception and meaning. Phenomenology rejects the notion of some undetermined or uninterpreted datum below the level of signification in our experience of the world. It turns instead to naive experience as its primary field of evidence. But from this primary field it seeks to thematize and extract those features of man's relationship with his surrounding world, those structural characteristics which allow an understanding of the mundanity in which we all operate. Phenomenology finds naive experience to be already rich and full—and the phenomenologist's task becomes the explication of that richness and the clarification of that significance in relation to the structural features of experience.

In the context of a phenomenology of eros, I want to begin my contribution by descriptively opening some of the aspects of *sense and sensuality* first in the area of touch perception. The turn to perception first, I would point out, is also a typically phenomenological move. The "primacy of perception" asserted by both Husserl and Merleau-Ponty is an always present focus of experience—we are focally perceptually engaged with the world.

The choice of touch phenomena as a prologue to the phenomenology of eros should be obviously appropriate. Touching in the most intimate sense is clearly sexual. But even as I begin two problems pose themselves: on the one hand I cannot retrace and outline all the conceptual machinery which I presuppose. The "tribal language" of phenomenology (epoché, the phenomenological reductions, eidetic intuition, etc.) would draw us too far afield for a short essay—so I deliberately take the risk of certain short-cuts which may result in misunderstandings. In my descriptions I shall deliberately take examples from ordinary experiences to point up what I am locating. Often from only one or two examples I will appear to generalize about some structural feature of experience. The danger which this shortcut faces is that I may leave the impression that phenomenology is a type of common sense philosophy which uses induction as its method—and that is not the case. I would therefore point out that my examples are carefully selected to illustrate points which are and should be arrived at only after widely ranging "perspective variations" from which "invariants" are "eidetically intuited." I can only hope to be suggestive for the non-phenomenologist and hope that the phenomenologists will forgive the shortcuts.

On the other hand the selection of touch as a sensory variable risks a very unphenomenological result. Our naive experience is first and foremost global—in our involvements with the surrounding world we normally do not select out a "sense" and, phenomenologically, the so-called five senses are already a kind of reflective abstraction. Nevertheless, I can clearly focus upon touch within this global experience—but I must be aware that I am already doing a first order reflection. My reason for beginning in this way is that by simplifying the examination in considering only one sensory variable a certain clarity may emerge more easily than might be the case otherwise. Thus I choose touch for the sake of initial simplicity, because of its clearly important role in sexuality, and because it quickly illustrates the clues to my fleshy embodiment in the world.

But as I begin to describe what occurs in touching I find myself immediately faced with the traditions of our cartesian heritage. The term, body, suggests an object, something objectified. And if I try to think of this objectification in perceptual and ordinary terms it might perhaps be thought that I-as-body am co-equal to an object, perhaps co-extensive with the visual outlines we perceive. Note that this *idea* we get of ourselves may well be drawn more from our experiences of others than it is of ourselves. We see him in profile—but we see only a very limited aspect of ourselves. We then may leap to the thought that I am "like" him—as a separate object-body. That more than this is involved even with the perception of others I need not point out here—but in this cartesian context I further apply to myself the notion that just as he appears to me without the full perspective of his "inner sense" so even more strongly may I think myself an object-body. Phenomenologically it makes all the difference *how* I gain whatever knowledge I have. In the case being described I would only point out that I never get a full detached perspective upon myself in the same way that I do upon the other. And secondly, I experience a full "inner sense" of myself in a way which is different from the apperceptions I gain of the other. The knowledge, the *idea*, I get of myself as "like" the other is not coextensive with the "feel" I have myself—nevertheless, the idea of myself as object may lead me to conclude certain things about what I *must* experience almost in spite of what I *do* experience.

This applies to the experience of touch. I might conclude, for example, that because my skin is presumably the place where "touch sensations" occur this must be the place where I actually feel—and this would mean that touch is not a distance sense. But in my role now as phenomenologist I "bracket" all such assumptions, inferences, and theories of causation in order to first turn to naive experience as it gives itself out. I must first locate myself in these acts.

First example: I find very quickly that my experience of touch does not at all remain within the confines of my body-as-outlined object, but I find in certain cases, indeed many, that I can feel and touch at a distance. The classic example is the blind man and his cane. He feels the sidewalk—at the end of his cane. Take a pencil and run it along the desk or the blackboard and take very careful note of where the feeling is (close your eyes if necessary) and you soon discover that the feeling is at the end of the pencil—or, better put, you feel the desk where the contact actually is—at the junction of pencil-desk. My sense of touch exceeds my bodily outline.

Even more remarkable is the skill developed by the physician. In the pencil example the surfaces were hard and perhaps surface and texture is what you first noted—but the doctor as he thumps upon you does not feel the surface so much as he feels your interior. The size of your heart, the configuration of your liver, the arrangement of organs or nodules are felt inside you. His touch penetrates the surface of your body to the interior.

The cartesian, of course, has elaborate ways of attempting to save his presuppositions when confronted with such odd, but ordinary experiences. His explanatory acrobatics attempt to continue his notion of sensation as "inside" and that which "really happens" as an unexperienced "outside." But in my present role I shall no longer argue with him, I merely turn to what the phenomenologist derives from these and similar experiences. These experiences illustrate the first feature of *intentionality*. Experience, consciousness, is consciousness *of* x. Experience refers, points to, is directed into the world. I feel the desk, the doctor feels the shape of my heart, the first reference of intentionality is the *Other*.

So much is the case that in our ordinary involvements with the world we hardly take notice of our feelings in any explicit sense at all. We are immersed in our projects. The blind man's feel for the sidewalk, although he is clearly aware of things that we overlook altogether, is secondary to his project of getting to where he is going. Return to the pencil on the desk example. In this case my direction located the project on the feeling itself—my question set the context. What "stood out" was the feeling of pencil-desk. We felt the desk as the doctor felt the size of my heart, and so on. Our experiences were focused. But a focus is a selection, an emphasis, a theme within the totality of experience. It is not all that is going on.

If I now ask you to repeat the experiment of the pencil on the desk and ask you what else you feel in addition to the first thing that stood out you would soon notice that you also feel—at one and the same time—a vague pressure on your fingers as the pencil traces its route on the desk. And by conscious effort you can even begin to make this finger-pencil aspect of the experience stand out. But when it does, the pencil-desk aspect tends to fade and vice-versa. While both aspects are present one tends to stand in the center of the vocus while the other fades to a fringe awareness.

Once again from these simple experiences I generalize to another structural feature of intentionality, the feature I call the *core/fringe structure*. Simply put, in ordinary consciousness we have a core of attention around which but at the same time are arranged a number of fringe experiences. I can vary this focus at will (or I may be called upon to switch its direction by some distraction) but in the normal situation, what is core "stands out" while what is fringe is only vaguely present.

Now let us begin to vary our examples farther. I lie down on a soft couch and begin to read. As I become absorbed in my reading the touch relationship between the couch and my backside begins to fade so far to the fringes of my consciousness that I find that I seem to be almost floating. The more usual sense of semi-weightiness which I feel when I walk or even when I sit down is replaced by this semi-weightlessness. As phenomenologist such an occurrence may become interesting and I switch my attention to it. Unlike the pencil example in which I was able to detect very precise differences in the object I was feeling through it, I find that the cloud-like couch-me experience is so vague that not even any clear distinction between me and where I end and couch is capable of being made. Inner and outer, subject and object are here not at all clear and distinct.

In the couch-me end of the continuum there lies a vagueness which perhaps disturbs some philosophers. I quickly rush to the other end of the continuum of touch phenomena and recall the experience of the safecracker: his deft fingers, sandpapered to supersensitivity, feel the fall of the tumblers inside. And the quality control man in a paperplant who, by letting the rapidly rolling ribbon of paper glide between his fingers, is able to detect even the slightest variance or imperfection. Surely here is clarity. Note, now, two things. First, phenomenologically, experientially speaking, any reference of attention is a positive phenomenon. I can concentrate and focus upon vagueness just as well as I can upon precision. Furthermore, there is no experiential reason to preclude one phenomenon being any more important than the other. Second, in the continuum of vagueness to precision of which our touch is capable of locating, I find that some areas of my bodily experience are more sensitive than others. In some respects I and world tend to merge, in others I am embodied precision through which I operate upon the world.

To this point and within the limits of ordinary experience we have noted that: (a) touching is intentional in the sense that its reference is the other. It is directed towards the other in the world; (b) within the totality of experience and within touch there is usually a focus which stands in inverse relation to those aspects of the touch experience which stand on the fringe. In this case, that which stands out is clearly present to my experience, while that which is on the fringe is barely noticed; (c) but there is also a continuum of feeling within the range of touch such that in some cases the other seems to merge with me in a vagueness which blurs the distinctions between subject and object—although at the other end of the continuum there may be a greatly refined precision in which I am able to detect the minutest differences of that which stands over against me.

Now, however, it is time to begin noting unique features. The central such feature of touch has long been noted as touch-touched: whenever I touch something I am also touched. Obviously, great differences occur between my initiation of a touch occurrence and one in which I am suddenly touched by another—but in both instances the contact is focalized in touch-touched. I touch the cold wall, and it touches me with its coldness. I touch the slippery vinyl of the contemporary art exhibit, and it touches me with its invented sensuality. I touch the warm flesh of my beloved and her flesh touches me with warmth. *This* is the lack of distance that is so often attributed to touch—it is not distance which makes the difference, it is the latent and *implied intimacy* of touch in a necessary mutuality which makes the difference. Touch in this respect is not quite like those dimensions of experience such as sight or hearing—not every time that I see am I seen nor am I spoken to every time I speak (although I do hear my own voice when I speak)—but every time I touch, I am also touched. There is a necessary mutual intimacy to touch.

We could have noticed this feature in any of the first examples: in touching the desk I am touched; in lying on the couch the pleasant semi-weightlessness creates its touch ambiguity; in touching the paper it touches me with its smoothness or roughness. All of this lies within the focal possibilities, there is a field of fringe features as well. Touch is also *total*, a plenum never empty of an overall intimate contact with the world. This field of touch is constant even though we are seldom explicitly aware of it.

There are at least two approaches to noting this feature of touch experience. One is by varying our focus within the touch field through a whole series of examples which gradually point up how broad and total our contact with the world through touch is. I note that I do have a fleeting or vague awareness of the fit inside my shoes and that when I walk I am aware at the fringes that the floor feels differently when it is carpeted and when it is not. I note that I do have a marginal consciousness of the touch of my collar and the feel of my coat upon my back. And as I explore these fringe perceptions I may even begin to note that there is a very faint feel of the air against my face which is usually a bit cooler than the feel of the rest of my body. And I may note that in some sense all these factors are present within the same period of time although I rarely pay attention to any or all of these features. There is a field of touch within which my specific touch attention is focused upon only some small and highly selected aspect.

But these field characteristics may also be discovered at a stroke, in a sudden *field state*. I plunge, as is my particular passion, into the trout brook in Vermont late in the evening. The almost icy water surrounds me—and I am acutely and instantaneously aware of that cold environment which embraces me. A little later when I emerge, the relative warmth of the evening air gives me a feeling of exhiliaration throughout my whole body. Still later as I sit before the outdoor fire I am also aware of the crispy warm feeling of my frontside while my backside begins again to feel the creeping cold of the evening. Finally, relaxed and no longer concerned with the projects of the day, I slip into bed and pull the soft sleeping bag around me and the whole of my bodily being is warm and comfortable.

In these examples the field states of touch become vividly clear. And in these experiences, when the whole of my touch field touches and is touched by the surrounding world, I realize how intimate is the I-world relation in touch. Through touch, I am constantly "in touch" with that which surrounds me. But also in these states it is difficult to say just where I end and world begins. All the specific touches found in focal attentiveness are never separate from total Touch as the constant field in which I live.

I deliberately selected enjoyable field states to first illustrate the touch plenum—however, there are also negative states which could be noted. As a boy on the farm, I recall that one of the most unpleasant such states occurred during the harvesting of oats. The chaff somehow was able, through the course of the day, to permeate my clothing and eventually turn the whole of my body into an itching, hot-sweaty misery. Wanting to escape this unbearable situation became my primary desire through the day and my greatest hope was that the barrel which contained water for a shower had been filled that morning. To rid oneself of a negative field bespeaks the potential horror of being immersed in a world not of one's choosing.

To this point I have tried to show that all touch displays a structural intimacy between me and the world. I am in constant touch with that surrounding world although I am so familiar with my usual surroundings that only on certain occasions—such as those which dramatically demonstrate field states—do I become aware of this total immersion in the touch field. More ordinarily, I am at best concerned with focused modalities of touch, the highlights and most obvious touch experiences which are located by my hands and feet—and as a professor, my seat. I would like to say that the touch world is like being in a presence of an ongoing symphony of many sound modalities—but that I usually pay attention only to the most obvious melodies.

I have noted that although touch seems to require some form of contact with its referential other, this contact in touching finds me touched. Its limits do not necessarily remain within the limits of my bodily outline. It is here that we arrive at the limit and artificiality of dealing with touch alone rather than global experience. I see textures, for example, and apperceptively "feel" them even though I don't literally touch them. Within global experience touch is thoroughly present.

The language of intimacy in touch has also been used deliberately. The structural and unavoidable intimacy of touch is clearly closely related to any serious attempt to deal with a phenomenology of eros. The arrangement or organization of the erotic is a complication upon all and every feature of touch perception. The relationship between touch and eros has long been partly understood in the suggestive metaphor: touch is the *language* of love. In some respects this is a good metaphor. If touch is the language of love, then it may be seen that this language has both surface and depth "grammars." It may be noted that language is extraordinarily complex, rich, and flexible just as are the possibilities of sexual touching. The "screaming curse" of a rape is a very different "word" from the gentle suggestion of invitation issued in the night my beloved makes in the barely perceptible movement. But both remain within the same language of touch and thereby the ambiguities of sexuality are already problematically announced. The rape is not without its intimacy any more than the lovers' couplings are without the possibilities of aggression and miscommunication.

Such a higher order phenomenon ought to give pause even to the most imaginative investigator so far as finding invariants is concerned. But the circle between touch and sexuality must begin to be closed. Thus by first making an initial connection between the richness of touch possibilities and the sexual orchestrations which are possible upon this basis, I move to the second dimension of the arrangement of touch distances. Intimacy in sexual touching is related to the whole of touch intimacy in the specific rites of invitation.

Between our touch and being touched lies the organization or the "constitution" of space in its concrete experiential form.

I choose to remain within the general confines of touch experience as I approach the subject of the erotic. I want to deal with a certain series of relationships with distance and invitation. A new theme would be entered if I turned from my previous emphasis upon my touching the other and changed the emphasis to that which touches me. In our life-world, after all, on many occasions it is the other who initiates or occasions the touch. These experiences can be disturbing.

I am walking in my dimly lit cellar seeking the right bottle of wine for the dinner and as I move into a corner the barely felt tingling of a spider web, followed by the delicate patter of feet on my cheek brings a shocking touch—I am touched by the unwanted otherness of the spider and his house and I quickly respond by brushing him off. I rid myself of this intrusion and place this creature at a proper distance from me. The spider has violated the sense of distance I wish to maintain. Between me and others, particularly strange or unfamiliar others, I pose an invisible barrier which is to be penetrated only by invitation or permission. I am not very unlike the lizard sunning himself on the wall who will ignore me until I come within that defense space—then he will dart into his hole.

The lifespace around is constituted space. It is filled with unspoken but definite senses of meaningful possibilities. And because touch is structurally intimate it is also well ordered according to these patterns of invitation or rejection, of rituals of acceptance or rites of warning.

I am an athlete, and leaving the locker I reach out and pat my teammate on the rump in a gesture of support and encouragement. But while I might never think of it, I know that I wouldn't do the same to my colleague as he prepares to enter the lecture hall. Or, I might give a friendly and light blow to the chest of a long forgotten high school friend—but I would hardly do the same to my secretary when she came back from vacation.

Our touching is intertwined with unseen but pregiven meanings. We carry with us an easily felt warning—do not penetrate too quickly or too closely unless you are invited. Of course, there are indefinitely many ways to structure our touching of one another—but these ways are constituted nevertheless. We may form a sensitivity group which evolves new understandings and within the protective confines of "our group" we may get to the point of taking off our clothes and huddling together—but only after having gone through the requisite rituals and never yet do we perform the same acts spontaneously with the saleslady in the department store. Our concrete existence is an ordered world in which we feel, more than know, how we may or may not touch.

Everything has its place in lifespace and he who does not have the implicit understanding of the concrete gesturings may cause misunderstanding or create violence. We introduce each other with the touch of two hands. But we talk to one another at a certain comfortable distance. An old Eastern European friend always made me feel uncomfortable as he thrust his face to within inches of mine to talk. And I would back away until the two or three feet of Western talking distance was reestablished. To me he seemed aggressive and threatening; to him I seemed to be rejecting his friendly desire to converse as comrade.

Sexuality, too, is organized and constituted within a context of implicitly understood arrangements of distance, invitation, and touch. This even in the most extreme examples. The prostitute would seem to be an example of non-organization of touch space. Anyone with the proper fee may touch her—but upon closer examination this is not at all the case. The fee is part of what plays the role of invitation ritual, a businesslike shortcut from our usual more complex rites of seduction. Moreover, to her the touch of her customer is very different from that of her lover-pimp. With the "john" or customer the touch is casual. She endures him and rarely experiences orgasm. Not so the relation with the lover-pimp—when he touches her it is "for real." Barbara Streisand's remark in the "Owl and the Pussycat" is perfectly appropriate with the context: "I may be a prostitute, but I'm not promiscuous." Even here the intimacy relations of touch are encircled and constituted through implicit languages of touch.

Thus to change the patterns of invitation and the role of touch in the erotic is also to change the meaning of sexuality. The experimentation which is now occurring in communes and on campuses illustrates this. On an ideological level the "new freedom" is conceived as actualizing a dream of human unity and equality which extends to sexual relations. And surely the boy or girl who live in this experiential context remain far from the context of the prostitute. In their case mutual invitation within a non-commercial context may occur; a certain type of satisfaction may occur—but if I read what happens correctly there are also antimonies which emerge in the change of pattern.

One factor relates back to the hard to destroy inheritance of a cultural double-standard which still pervades our society. With an abundance of "easy chicks" today's male finds it simple to regress to a crude level of self-satisfaction without a sense of mutuality in relation to his partner. Marx, a century ago, realized that free love in a communal situation could be a merely communal way of treating women as chattel.

A second factor is closely related to the first. If the metaphor of a language is maintained, public or even group language remains a step removed from the subtle complexities of intimate lovers' language. Thus one hears more and more about the breadth of sexual experience and less and less about intimate sensuality—"I've balled lots of chicks, but haven't found many I could love." Non-selective or widely selective sexuality becomes a bit like shaking hands—there are those who grip you strongly with expression of character and others who touch like cold flounders. And while it is impolite to refuse the shaking of hands with anyone, it is more difficult for me to imagine having to share beds with the sexual equivalent of the flounder.

The point I am making is a structural, not an ethical one. The possibilities of multiple dialects within the totality of sexual language is so great as to stagger the imagination. But at the same time within a language or any dialect the most subtle meanings are not generally conferable. What is common remains inverse to what is exceptional. The subtle meanings, hidden significations, much that is unsaid, may easily be conveyed in a dialogue between friends, within small circles, and most clearly between persons who have had the longest and most intimate contacts. This indirect communication *is* possible to a degree even in some wider situations, but not in the same way. To choose one type of language situation as normative is to exclude another, but to choose is unavoidable.

The complexity of our rituals of invitation and the possibilities of organization of our touch relationships is staggering—but they are nonetheless constituted within the varied contexts of pregiven significations. Sexual intimacy unfolds within the "logic" of these contexts. But after all this is said there still seems to remain a sense of primordial privilege to sexual touching. Even apart from the mysteries of desire the full intimacy of touch within sexuality is heightened so that this act stands out among acts of touch.

After the invitation has been issued and accepted, the lovers came together in a play of the full orchestration of touch perception. To overcome the invisible barrier of protection, to invite the other to touch you in this way, to be open to one another, is also to bring into play the full range of touch structures. Two persons, long familiar with one another, who understand the innuendos in the unspoken dialects of touch, retire from the day to end up face to face. Here no elaborate project of seduction nor any complex ritual of invitation is needed because both have long understood the slight movements which say without words.

Disengaged from the worries of the day this retirement into seclusion lessens the ordinary concentration upon the affairs which normally so occupy us that we are likely to miss those fringe phenomena which surround us and give richer texture to experience. The couple, relaxed, enter the bed and bring their flesh together. The disengagement from walking concerns and the surrounding warmth of the situation elicits a field state. The couple embrace through mutual invitation—I surround her and she me with as much of our bodies as possible. In this embrace as we surround each other we maximize the ambiguities of mutuality. We "float"—not unlike the experiences which lower the self-other distinctions—upon each other so that this vagueness of me-other is positively heightened.

Within this context, modulated by the pleasant field state and its me-other ambiguity, further tonalities may emerge. Those sensitive parts of ourselves, within the present and total field, are the focal themes which while not displacing the field state add to it in the symphony of sexuality. But even in these intense moments, even through the focus of the sexual act, the ambiguity of me-other continues. Only the conscious project of the refusal to communicate, to retire into oneself, makes this act alienated. If I inhabit my acts, if I am embodied in the fullness of touch perception, then in this symphonic moment with all of the features of touch fully alive I no longer contact the surface of the other; I live in and with the other.

Now I have opened a way which I never thought I would open. But I have left unsaid more than I have said. Positively, I have pursued a line of thought which sees the fullness of touch expressed in heightened form in sexual touch. The always present and implied intimacy of touch is here explicit and thorough. But this occurrence happens within a complex and highly ordered set of lived spatial configurations. The possibilities of communicative mutuality, implied in touch, are fragile. And although I intend to indicate that the nuanced sexual activity of the lovers who have learned something of the fullness of their "language" of love is a focal possibility; it is also clear that others less nuanced possibilities occur. But if the door to a further exploration of touch within a phenomenology of eros has opened even a little, I shall remain satisfied.

PART II.
LANGUAGE

CHAPTER NINE

Rationality and Myth

How can a philosopher understand myth in such a way as to be fair to the meaning of the myth without abandoning his own demands for rational rigor and clarity? In dealing with this question three steps are taken: (1) I argue that the two predominant interpretations of the relation of philosophy to mythology are wanting in important respects. A third way, proposed by Paul Ricoeur, shows more promise. (2) I then propose modifications to Ricoeur's suggestions which form the basis for a theory of myth which does not exclude rational analysis. (3) Through the comparison of myth and rationality certain implications become clear for the relation of myth and philosophy.

CLEARING THE WAY

Of the varied interpretations of the rise of philosophy out of a background of religio-mythological thought two predominant traditions seem to hold sway. The first follows a "windelbandian" thesis which pictures the rise of philosophy as a struggle to free rational thought from the bonds of myth in order to arrive at a critical and scientific mode of thought. In this interpretation the distinctions between myth and philosophy are quite sharply drawn and a definite valuation is accorded philosophy over myth. The "windelbandian" tends to view myth as an historical curiosity which may be interesting, but it is now to be relegated to the dead past. The "windelbandian" thesis *demythizes the history of philosophy.*

The second tradition follows an "eliadean" thesis which accepts the rather severe distinctions between philosophical rationality and religio-mythological thought forms. The "eliadeans," however, reverse the valuation. For them mythology preserves a certain sense of wholeness, unity, and innocence between man and his world which was lost once a critical and analytic mode of thought was introduced. Despite this nostalgia for myth, "eliadeans" recognize that once philosophical rationality has been introduced one can no longer return to the innocence of the myth as myth. This places the "elidean" in the position of other desiring a remythized philosophy.

Both "windelbandians" and "elideans" agree that there is a rather great gulf between philosophy and myth and both agree that the myth as myth has been lost. (The difference is that the first mutters, "good riddance," while the second sighs, "too bad.") But is this the end of the matter?

There has been an attempt at a third way. Paul Ricoeur has placed into serious question both of the theses mentioned. Against the 'eliadeans' Ricoeur argues that the world of myth is not so much an expression of wholeness, unity, and innocence as it is a vast attempt to attain these goals. The primitive mythologist is already separated and 'fallen' from nature.[1] The fact that he must dramatically rehearse some primordial connection with his world, must remind himself of it, is evidence of a distance rather than sheer intimacy. The mythologist symbolizes—he is already in the human world of language rather than in the pre-human world of merely 'being' nature. Thus even if one could return to the taking of myth as myth it would not be the rediscovery of an Eden.

Against the 'windelbandians' Ricoeur argues that there remains a certain suggestive richness to mythological expression which gives myth the characteristic of exercising a tenacious hold upon the imaginations of men.[2] It is a fact, after all, that certain myths have been repeated, renewed, and re-interpreted over vast stretches of human history. Adam Prometheus, and Faust, to mention a few, are still around in one form or another. Such tenacity has led some so far as to postulate a 'collective

---

1. Paul Ricoeur, *Philosphie de la Volonté*, Tome II: *Finitude et Culpabilité, La Symbolique du Mal* (Paris: Aubier, Editions montaigne, 1960), pp. 11, 16, 325.
2. *Ibid.*, p. 324.

unconsciousness' for the race of man. One might also argue that at least some philosophies have invented their own myths.

Ricoeur's third way calls for a *demytholization* rather than either demythizing or remythizing. This is another way of saying that the philosophical exploration of myth is the delicate task of seeking the basic meaning of the myth without returning to a pre-critical mode of thought. There must at least be a creative tension between rational thought and myth.

Ricoeur agrees with both 'windelbandians' and 'eliadeans' that the myth as myth is lost. As he puts it, for the modern critical man myth is *only* myth.[3] However, in a unique twist, Ricoeur argues that this 'loss' of myth as more than mere myth may prove to be the very means for the recovery of myth in its proper dimensions.[4]

The reason for this hope is due to the fact that critical thought may discern at least two types of intentionality in its *logos* or rational structure.[5] The function of the rational structure of the myth is to explain something. I shall paraphrase this function as the *literal significance* of the myth. The literal significance of the myth includes any model of the universe (as three storied, as a flat disk floating upon infinite seas, etc.) and any explanations of what we might call empirical phenomena (the biblical story of the tower of Babel 'explains' why there are many languages). It is this element of myth which is irretrievably lost.

This could, of course, be agreed upon by both major interpretations mentioned. However, certain errors might be committed at this point. A 'windelbandian' error might be to recognize and emphasize the rather vast distinction between what would count as explanation in a mythological context and what would be required for philosophical explanation. He would obviously hold to the superiority of the latter. The error which might occur arises out of the temptation to think that the myth is no more than a primitive attempt at explanation and thus the 'windelbandian' might toss out the myth with the outdated cosmology. This is an error which confuses one dimension of myth with its totality. At the very least this demythization overlooks the peculiar ability of myth to outlive its strict historical context. Despite losing its explanatory func-

---

3. *Ibid.*, p. 13.
4. *Ibid.*, p. 13.
5. *Ibid.*, p. 25.

tion the myth may still hold sway over the imagination. (One might also point with some alarm to the rather rapid way in which the literal truth about the world changes as well!)

In order to recognize what is lost and what is not lost and thus avoid this error, Ricoeur 'brackets out' any explanatory function of myths. This counts as a methodological device for all demythologizing.[6] This raises the question, what is left of the myth? Ricoeur's answer is that a second level of significance emerges from the myth once its literal significance is bracketed. The philosophical gain is the recovery of the *mythos* or symbolic function of the myth. I rephrase this the *imaginative significance* of the myth.

The symbolic function of myth is the portrayal of a certain situation of man in relation to the Sacred (or what he takes as the Sacred).[7] In other words, the imaginative significance of the myth is an interpretation of man's situation in the world. This is dramatized in the myth as a symbol of man's existence in relation to his ultimate destiny.

This dramatic picture of interpretation of man's existential situation is more than picture according to Ricoeur. It is also a means by which man orients himself in his life. The myth as a symbol exercises a directive function.

> Mythos means work; the imagination, insofar as it is a mythopoetic function, is also the seat of a profound laboring which controls the decisive changes in our vision of the world. Every real conversion is first a revolution on the level of our directive images. By changing his imagination, man changes his existence.[8]

Ricoeur obviously does not view imaginative significance as something trivial, nor by extension does he consider myth as a mere historical curiosity.

Yet on the other side of the issue Ricoeur does not want to remythize the world of thought. His own conclusions border upon a 'peaceful coexistence' between two types of thought. At the end of LA SYMBOLIQUE DU MAL Ricoeur meditates upon the relation of myth and

---

6. *Ibid.*, pp. 13, 328.
7. *Ibid.*, p. 13.
8. Paul Ricoeur, " 'The Image of God' and the Epic of Man," *Cross Currents*, translated by George Gringas, Vol. XI (Winter, 1961), 49.

philosophy. The key idea to his interpretation of this relation is found in the phrase, "Le symbole donne a penser."[9]

Myths, Ricoeur concludes, contain a certain suggestive wealth in their portrayal of human existence which cannot be merely reduced to rational form. Ricoeur characterizes this wealth which is to be a source for philosophical reflection as *opaque*.[10] Myth "donates" or contributes to rational thinking themes which have a certain power to reveal hidden dimensions of human existence. The philosopher is well advised to examine this wealth.

A THEORY OF MYTH

At this point I take leave of Ricoeur in any strict sense (although the following thesis does not run so much counter to Ricoeur as it does tangential). Ricoeur is not alone, of course, in noting the enigmatic suggestiveness of myth with its ability to direct the imaginations of men in various historical eras. To term this enigma opaque may even be an advance over the more usual and somewhat negative notion of ambiguity.

However, I suggest that opacity may be a bit too strong a term. It seems to suggest some 'insoluable mystery' which in turn may lead one to conclude that by its very nature myth is not entirely open to rational analysis. In order not to close the door to such a rational analysis in advance I would like to suggest that the source of the mythological opacity is due to the nature of myth as a *multi-dimensioned structure*. This is to say, from an already rationalistic point of view, that the hidden wealth of myth is due to its ability to contain several dimensions of meaning.

This model for understanding myth does not exclude the possibility of a thorough rational analysis of myth—but at the same time preserves a suggestion which accounts for the exceptional difficulty encountered by the analyst in dissecting myth. To make this claim is to imply various characteristics belong to rationality in distinction on the myth from the very beginning. (I undertake this question in the third section of the paper.)

---

9. Ricoeur, *La Symbolique du Mal*, p. 324.
10. *Ibid.*, p. 22. Cf. Paul Ricoeur, "The Hermeneutics of Symbols and Philosophical Reflections," *International Philosophical Quarterly*, translated by Denis Savage, Vol. II (May, 1962), 194.

To think of myth as a structure containing several dimensions of meaning may be helpful in several ways. First, one can argue that many of the usual interpretative problems concerning myth may arise from the failure to recognize the multi-dimensionality of myth. For example, the 'windelbandian' error of demythizing is probably due, not to a failure of rationality, but to the taking of a valid rational insight for the whole picture. It is not the case that the myth does not contain a literal significance and that this is quite distinct from that of scientific thought. Nor is it true that the relative superiority of the latter may be demonstrated. The error is due to the attempt to *reduce* all levels of myth-meaning to a single one. To reduce the myth is to distort it beyond recognition. One can very well imagine similar errors from a 'freudian,' for example, who validly discerns a certain sexual dimension to myth, but who then goes on to reduce the myth to a mere expression of some libidinous desire.

The second advantage of the multi-dimensioned model of myth has is that it recognized the complexity of the myth. Again, the problem is not the impossibility of rational analysis so much as the sheer size and complexity of the task. The 'mystery' of the myth, in this model, is not opacity, but the complexity of performing a series of rational analyses, each directed towards a single dimension of meaning. The primary questions here revolve around methods of procedure and the keeping straight of one's categories.

To put it another way, the problems which emerge from myth are not those which would deny 'truth' to the myth, but those which arise from an excess of 'truths' in the myth. From a multi-dimensioned structure one can only undertake a whole series of explications rather than a single one. The task here is making explicit what is implicit.

In some degree, therefore, the level one investigates depends upon the function one is out to isolate. I take it this is what Ricoeur is out after in his analyses of the various types of myths. The symbolic function is taken as a primary function—but this is merely to isolate one dimension without denying others.

In each case, however, the rational analyst does not take the myth in the strict sense of the term. He has already shifted his point of view from the literal significance of the myth (even if he is investigating the literal significance of the myth). What the model of myth as a multi-dimensioned structure provides is a working hypothesis for the rational investigator.

Such a model, however, is insufficient. As a matter of fact the multi-dimensioned structures of meaning within a myth are not even its central characteristic. Balancing the series of levels of meaning as a second characteristic is what might be called a certain mythological *clarity*. If one takes the model of multi-dimensionality as characteristic of myth, then one may say that the myth also unites the various levels of meaning into a single whole. Indeed, one difference between myth and rational thought is precisely that the myth 'says' what it has to say quickly, dramatically, and imaginatively—its many meanings are contained in a single container. This clarity of myth has often been overlooked.

Mythological clarity is the unique characteristic of making a whole series of dimensions of meaning 'fall together' into a coherent and dramatic picture. In turn this dramatic picture performs a *gestalt-function* for the imagination. This function may be illustrated in a fairly prosaic fashion. Often in teaching one will have listed a number of abstract ideas and attempted to explain their relations and implications to the students—only to be greeted in return by a blank look. But then a brilliant illustration occurs to you; it is told; and glimmers replace blankness. "Now I see what you mean!" The Illustration (myth, tale, etc.) makes the whole fall into place. It does not do away with the separate elements so much as it arranges and *orders* them into a complete gestalt.

That may have been what Plato understood in creating his own 'myths.' I would wager that the allegory of the cave more likely captures the imagination and is the occasion for remembering and explicating the complexities of the divided line than vice versa. Myth functions in a similar way by presenting in easily remembered form a series of basic ideas. Of course the illustrations I have used are reversed, since in those cases the story makes the series of already explicated ideas fall into place. A myth 'contains' the ideas and part of the task of rational analysis is to make these explicit.

Not only does mythological clarity function as a gestalt; it also can be seen in a basically democratic appeal to the imagination. The simple man as well as the educated man can 'understand' the myth (even if at different levels). It is this characteristic which may partly account for the lasting quality of myth and perhaps also for its use as a symbol of cultural unity. One may return again and again to the myth in its imaginative significance. In it, over and over again, some basic point or interpretation of man's existence may be seen.

To this point I have dwelt upon characteristics of myth which might be considered structural. While these characteristics might be considered necessary conditions for the ability of myth to function as it does in human history they are not sufficient conditions.

Sufficient conditions are harder to describe and analyze (and are basically outside the scope of this paper). However one can return to Ricoeur's contention that myths serve a symbolic and existential function here. That is, the themes which make myths a source for thinking are basic ones for the questions of human existence. Birth, death, evil, salvation, the mystery of the world, man's fate, all of these are the issues which form the substance of mythological themes. An extended study of myths would isolate a number of ideal types and explication could begin at this point.[11] One might further speculate that a primary myth was one which coalesces certain basic existential problems of human existence into a single coherent theme, expressing in clarity and with the sense of depth acquired from the multiple dimensions of meaning a basic interpretation of man's existence.

MYTH AND RATIONALITY

To this point I have been primarily concerned with clearing a way towards a philosophical analysis of myth and with a rudimentary outline of a theory of myth. There have been throughout certain implications for the structure of rationality and myth which have not been made explicit. If myth has implications for philosophy, then the reverse is also the case. It may be through a mutual comparison of philosophical rationality and myth that certain insights may now be made clear.

I hold that both philosophy and myth have their own types of clarity and both exercise an ordering function. However, the basic model for each type of clarity and ordering is distinct. A series of comparisons may help illustrate what I have in mind.

(a) The models of clarity in myth and rationality are quite polarly distinct. I have indicated that while a rational analysis of myth is not in principle impossible, it is an exceedingly bulky and complex job. This is due to the two quite different types of clarity. *Mythological clarity is multi-dimensioned; rationality is mono-dimensioned.* Mythological clarity is achieved in a dramatic picture which 'says' what it has to say calls

---

11. This is the primary task to which Ricoeur addresses himself in *La Symbolique du Mal.*

for a whole series of analyses. Rationality, in contrast, achieves its clarity by taking a single idea at a time and following out its implications to logical conclusions.

(b) These two types of clarity also have correlative differing types of modeling or ordering procedures. The myth to be effective cannot be long, overly detailed, too complicated, etc. The story must have a plot which is simple enough to catch the imagination and hold it. The myth serves as *symbol*. Rationality, on the other hand, drives towards *system*. At best it takes an idea and builds upon or around this idea a well-knit structure (for example, Spinoza's ETHICS constitute one of the most theoretically 'beautiful' systems in the history of philosophy).

(c) One might say, though with qualifications, that myth makes use of many dimensions of meaning implicit in its structure to make *one point*. All of the drama revolves around a central major theme (life is tragic and men suffer at the hands of the gods, etc.) Rationality takes one theme and uses it to make many points. Myth is condensed; rationality is dispersed.

(d) In short, mythological power is found in its ability to order the imagination. The directive aim is to provide a concrete symbol for some major interpretations of a life situation. Philosophical power is found in its ability to order reasoning with the aim of displaying a clear and logically connected structure in a lineal way.

These comparisons, however, only illustrate the already accepted distinction between philosophizing and mythologizing. The question remains as to how philosophy relates to myth. I have two concluding suggestions:

First, the job of philosophical analysis may be directed toward myth. But in any actual analysis the rationality of that analysis is both *more than* and *less than* the content of the myth which it explicates.

It is more than the myth in the sense that analysis can isolate and bring to rational awareness the various ideas implicit in the myth. And once isolated the idea can be exhibited and extended to its logical conclusion. In this sense a rational analysis of myth is an 'archeology.' It digs out the implicit meanings and clarifies the myth.

On the other hand the analysis is also less than the myth. The analysis cannot replace the myth. To so think would be akin to replacing a work of art with the criticisms which had been performed upon it. Even after the separate analyses are performed one cannot merely claim to have exhausted the myth as such. One may have exhausted it rationally, but analysis does not exercise the gestalt-function of the myth. In this sense analysis is like a translation—something is always lost even if it isn't the clarity of the idea.

Second, once rational analysis has begun one never returns to the myth purely and simply. The 'loss' variously evaluated by 'windelbandian,' 'eliadeans,' and now 'ricoeureans' remains lost. If we take the 'ricoeurean' line, however, this cannot be considered a loss as such. It is rather a shift in mode of understanding. If I were positivistically inclined I might refer to this shift of mode as a shift from the material to the formal mode. This seems a bit inappropriate to the subject matter, rather I would suggest that philosophically one views myth from an 'aesthetic' rather than a 'religious' understanding.

By this I mean that one cannot live in the world of myth as such. Myth cannot be taken as literally significant and therefore cannot call for our firmest commitment. One can live, as Ricoeur puts it, in the 'aura' of the myth.[12] One can take the myth as a significant symbol which can be appreciated and even used within limits as a directive form. But one cannot return to the world of myth in a post-mythological age. This is to reaffirm that at least certain important dimensions of myth are historical curiosities while other dimensions are not. But even those which have lasting imaginative significance must be taken provisionally.

All of this may leave us with an enigma—what is to be taken as literally significant today? And is what we so take in actually the myth of the 20th century? This seems to me a question worth investigation in a critical age and its form may well arise out of a philosophical investigation of myths.

---

12. Ricoeur, "The Hermeneutics of Symbols," p. 202.

CHAPTER TEN

Language and Two Phenomenologies

I have three concurrent concerns in this chapter. The first is to display a picturable model of some of the main features of phenomenological method. I wish in this case to clarify some of the complexities and implications of a phenomenological procedure for a philosophical context often more Anglophilic and Europophobic than not. But on the way to this end I wish also to begin the sketch of what I hope will become a considered re-interpretation of phenomenological history. I wish to differentiate two distinguishable, but often confused, lines of development from a common base in Husserlian thought. These types of phenomenology may be called respectively, existential phenomenology, and hermeneutic phenomenology, and are initiated in their essential forms respectively by Maurice Merleau-Ponty and Martin Heidegger. And thirdly I wish to indicate briefly how the question of language lies embedded in these distinctions. My outline of phenomenological development, then, wishes to account for the recent and increasing interest in the philosophy of language currently displayed among phenomenologists.

And since the tradition of European born philosophies of consciousness are often given to excesses of self-consciousness, I shall remain true to form and bring to public awareness some underlying polemic concerns as well. Permit me three gross generalizations: (a) Existentialism, as it has been understood particularly on this Continent, in a quasi-literary and often romantic guise is all but dead philosophically. This was the common opinion among the French professors I talked to in recent years, and although death throes may last longer just as birth pains start later in the USA, the symptoms are beginning to appear here, too. Herzog in the novel of the same name (and still placing Heidegger in the existential category) proclaims that, "We must get beyond Heidegger." (b) But this is not to say that existentialism in more philosophical form is dead. Quite to the contrary, as existential *phenomenology* it is just now beginning to make its appearance. As Sartre and Camus recede, Merleau-Ponty emerges. The previous guilt by association with the cultically "very existential" is replaced by concerns with more philosophically traditional problems revolving around perception, the problem of the body, and language. (c) Despite the difficulty in dissociating the popular meaning of existentialism from its philosophical basis and the even more difficult task of removing Heidegger from that category, I would point out that today most Europeans are beginning to argue that Heidegger is actually and not just polemically correct when he disclaims ever having been an existentialist.

To counter these historical misconceptions and to construct a reinterpretation which apologetically helps to point up the properly philosophical dimensions of phenomenology, I wish to propose a new tripartite framework of understanding. Again permit me three general points: (a) Since all phenomenology in its most precise and recent formulation forms a constellation around Edward Husserl in spite of the countergravitational pulls of Hegel, Kant, and Descartes, not to speak of Hume, I propose that we begin to think of phenomenology as a movement from Husserl to various forms of neo-Husserlianism. (b) To date the main lines of two distinguishable directions of neo Husserlian phenomenology are *existential* and *hermeneutic* phenomenologies. Merleau-Ponty most clearly exemplifies the first and Heidegger I now wish to cast into the second type. (c) Both of these developments have sources in the central and original phenomenological model developed by Husserl and particularly from the two sides of his notion of intentionality as the main structure of consciousness. Paul Ricoeur, one of the foremost Husserl interpreters, gives us the key from which I extend my interpretation. He says:

> "In Husserl's first works ... consciousness is defined not by perception, that is to say by its very presence to things, but rather by its distance and its absence. This distance and absence are the power of signifying, of meaning ... Thus consciousness is doubly intentional, in the first instance by virtue of being a signification and in the second instance by virtue of being an intuitive fulfilling.

In short, in the first works, consciousness is at once speech and perception."[2]

In my interpretative extension of this observation I wish to show that existential phenomenology draws its strength from what I shall call the implicit perceptualism of Husserl's concept of intentionality. Thus, although using radically different interpretations, existential phenomenology has motivations not unlike those of empiricism.

In contrast, I wish to show that hermeneutic phenomenology draws its concern from problems of language, also inherent in Husserl's concept of intentionality. This development is most clearly evident in Heidegger's work. It is a use of phenomenology which turns to problems of history and culture and which tends to read experience and ultimately perception itself in terms of a tradition of interpretation.

To outline this interpretation I turn first to a description of a general phenomenological model as a type of reflective philosophy. This type of model has its roots in the Husserlian origins of phenomenology and as a general model is the origin upon which variations are worked.

PHENOMENOLOGICAL MODELS: WE DO IT WITH MIRRORS ...

Reflective philosophies with parentage in the line of Descartes, Kant and Hegel before Husserl, usually are described as philosophies of consciousness or sometimes as subjectivisms. But often what is involved with reflection is not clarified as a methodological notion. Reflection in our language may mean some contemplative or re-thinking activity—or it may mean more literally a reflection from a mirror or another reflective surface. My entry into a description of phenomenological reflection lies in a deliberate choice of what I would like to call *the metaphor of the mirror*. When asked how I do phenomenology, I reply, I do it with mirrors. Because, as we shall see, in both thinking as reflection and the reflection from the mirror what is arrived at is done so *indirectly*.

In fact, the metaphor of mirror may first help clarify a persistent confusion among many who first read phenomenological descriptions as if they were simply revivals of introspective psychology. The key to the

---

1. Ricoeur, Paul: *Husserl* (Northwestern University Press), p. 210.

difference lies not in the material dealt with, since phenomenology deals with both so-called introspective contents and extrospective contents, but with the use of reflective indirectness.

To further precise this model I wish to introduce an analogy between the "I" and "eye." In relation to the history of epistemology with its play upon the subject and the object, phenomenology is a method which strictly reduces or restricts itself to a relational or bi-polar understanding of the subject and the object. Husserl's *ego-cogito-cogitatum,* Heidegger's *In-der-Welt-sein,* and Merleau-Ponty's *Etre-au-monde* are all versions of this essential characteristic of phenomenological method.

Thus a rule for phenomenology is that there is no subject without a corresponding object nor is there a knowable object except for and related to a subject. This insistence upon maintaining a relational scheme is actually the functional heart of Husserl's so-called transcendental idealism. But its theoretical function serves as a normative concept which differentiates phenomenology from both the classical realist and idealist frameworks. The *epoche* or phenomenological reduction, understood in this light, is the means of strictly maintaining the bi-polarity and "bracketing" the work in relation to speculative metaphysics. The aim is to suspend presuppositions, not experience.

This suspension of belief is on one side anti-realist in the sense that phenomenology brackets the idea of an existent which exists apart from experience. But functionally this suspension merely establishes all contents of experience as "objects," or better, object-correlates *for* experience in order that they be displayed for description prior to fitting them into an explanatory or constructive schema. All cogitata or contents of experience become noema or object-correlates and are to be considered only in their relations to a subject. This means that the implied theory of evidence which takes shape in Husserl's philosophy is one which weights all immediate of fulfillable experiences as prior to constructions. In this sense phenomenology is potentially open from its very beginning to an "empiricist" direction—but an empiricism which remains distinct from its British and American relations in several ways.

But if realist assumptions are bracketed by the strict reduction to relationality, the same goes for classical idealism. The ego or the I nowhere exists in pehnomenology without a world or field of contents which are the object correlates. Thus Husserl's supposed idealism must again be seen as a methodological function rather than the assertion of the primacy of mind. Unlike, or short of Descartes, Husserl's suspension of the world is not an active doubt, but a suspension of presuppositions concerning how the world is given out to be. The world is always to be described as it gives itself out to be to the knowing subject.

In both these senses the first central feature of the pehnomenologically reduced model is the strict maintenance of a relationality between the I and the world. Once this reduction is presupposed, the metaphor of the mirror with its analogy may be re-introduced as follows:

The eye is to the mirror
(or reflective surface)
as the I is to the World

And if we were to ask the question: how does the eye see itself or the I understand itself? The answer will be, only reflectively or indirectly. It sees itself as reflected in the mirror and I understand myself through the world.

This question, in its Husserlian context, establishes the *order* of procedure. Husserl's descriptions begin with the noematic or object-correlates of the relation. Thus in the metaphor of the mirror what is first noted is that which appears immediately or naively "out there" as the appearance in the mirror. The naive level of awareness is always first directed to what is "out there" or in the world. This choice is one which makes a certain degree of sense in relation to both the history of civilization and the history of the individual. The pre-scientific aborigine and the preacculturated child may not be aware of our usual inner-outer distinctions, but they are aware of a certain "objectivity" to appearances. Thus dreams and spirits as well as rocks and trees are "objective" in the sense that they are "out there" as they appear to the individual. Phenomenology takes this pre-theoretical naivete to its extreme in the description of a layer of experience later called the *lifeworld* in Husserl's writings. Thus under the restrictions of the reduction the first focus is upon the contents of experience as they give themselves out to be primitively. What appears in the mirror is first to be described.

But in the case of the metaphor of the mirror a complication is entered. The face directly before the mirror is mine and the eye reflects my eye. A turn may be made to the subject as the experiencer—but made by means of the reflection. Again the history of the individual and the civilization display in rough outline such a turn. The child at some point learns to recognize himself in the mirror, the reflection is seen as a reflection of himself in a level of awareness perhaps never attained by the parakeet. It is from the reflection, the bouncing off from the object-correlate, that the eye is to be seen, and it is from the experience of the world that the I is to be understood.

It is precisely this reflective turn which differentiates Husserl at one blow from Hume whom he admired so strongly. Husserl's critique of Hume's introspective psychology which finds itself unable to find a subject is located in the lack of a reflective turn. The ego does see itself-reflectively. From this phenomenological indirectness Husserl attempts to establish the structures of experienc*ing* upon the experienc*ed*.

It is well known that the structure of *intentionality* became the key concept around which the understanding of experience was elaborated in the Husserlian sense. Revolving around this central concept were a cluster of other notions such as "horizons," the "ray" of attention, and passive and active syntheses. But again it is the relationality of object and subject polarity which establishes this structure. Here we may put together both moments of the metaphor of the mirror.

If I first look at the mirror and observe carefully I can note that the whole of the appearing surface is one which does not ordinarily appear with a flat or equal value. Usually somewhere near the center of the mirror the phenomena "stand out" while those on the fringe are less explicit. The eye spots the eye looking back. And if I were able to remain completely restricted to a naive and probably hypothetical level of awareness I would end up saying that the center of objects in my field of vision are "more real" or "more important" than those at the edge. But even in an ordinary context the reflective turn is already made and I say instead that my *attention* is what is focused. It is I who "make stand out" what I will under my gaze. Permit me here to make several leaps and conclude at the risk of prematurely losing specifics that this notion of a ray of attention within a wider or surrounding field becomes a picturable model for the general structure of experience in the Husserlian context. Experience is not only selective in the normal case, but displays itself as directional or referential.

But more important in the present context is the fact that the structure of experiencing is established by means of the reflective turn, and all experiencing is to be read via or upon the world of appearances. There is no subjectivity, phenomenologically speaking, apart from a world. But what is initially taken as a reflective surface makes a great deal of difference.

MULTIPLE "WORLDS" OR THE HALL OF MIRRORS

From a description of a general model based upon an interpretation of Husserl, I move to its variants with the neo-Husserlians. Husserl himself evolved a number of ways towards phenomenology, and he characterized himself as a beginner to the end of his days. At least three of these ways to phenomenology have become watermarks in traditional Husserl interpretations. The so-called "early Husserl" found his way to phenomenology by means of *eidetic* sciences, i.e., mathematical and logical questions, and in this period he belongs to the set of philosophers who were concerned with the problems of logicism and psychologism at the turn of the century. The "middle Husserl," particularly of the *Cartesian-Meditations* tried for a while to describe phenomenology as a type of egology modeled in certain respects upon a Cartesian paradigm—but with some essential differences. It was during this period that the questions of solipsism were at their height. The "late Husserl" began to take a third major direction, increasingly perceptualistic in its form in the concept of the *lifeworld*. It is here that he comes closest to what was to become an *existential* phenomenology.

I shall not enter into the various arguments in current Husserl scholarship which now often revolve around this enigmatic period other than to make two suggestive indications about possible relations to the neo-Husserlians I shall momentarily examine. First, it is possible and perhaps even likely that Heidegger, already published and working out his own phenomenology, may well have influenced Husserl himself in relation to the *lifeworld* concept. Secondly, it is demonstrably the case that Merleau-Ponty concentrated his work upon the so-called "late Husserl" and took the lifeworld as a primary concept in the development of his own version of phenomenology.

Rather I shall return to the structurally generalized model I have suggested and indicate how the neo-Husserlians began to vary this model to their own uses. The differentiation into an existential and a hermeneutic phenomenology depends upon which of the dual foci of consciousness is taken as primary, perception or signification, upon which serves as a "world." Thus, if I maintain my mirror metaphor, what is taken as the reflective surface is of great importance. I shall argue that although there are obvious overlaps between existential and hermeneutic phenomenologies that Merleau-Ponty makes use of a "perceptual mirror" and Heidegger a "linguistic mirror." I shall, however, deal with these variants in an order inverse to their actual history since I believe that in some respects Merleau-Ponty comes closer to an extension of Husserl than Heidegger who couples phenomenology with a quite different set of problems than those motivating Husserl.

Existential phenomenology as a perceptualist philosophy

Merleau-Ponty began with the "late Husserl" who had already turned increasingly to problems of perceptual experience. It was a turn which, accelerated in Merleau-Ponty's thought, formed the possibility for existential phenomenology. Merleau-Ponty put it bluntly: "Far from being, as one might think, the formula for an idealist philosophy, the phenomenological reduction is that of an existentialist philosophy."[2] But in turn, an existential philosophy is one which focuses upon and makes more explicit the perceptualist side of Husserl's basic model. The distance to the world of the "early Husserl becomes the presence to the world (Etre-au-monde) of Merleau-Ponty.

But a perceptualism was implicit from the beginning in Husserl's theory of evidence. For one thing the very use of language in Husserl drew its strength from perceptual metaphor. The phenomenological process was described as "viewing phenomena"; experience was focused as a "ray of attention"; things appeared in "perspective variations"; and even introspection was termed "inner perception." But more essentially, the whole reduction was one which as a theory of evidence increasingly weights immediacy or concrete experience as primary. Only that which is "bodily present" or which can be fulfilled in the intuition (experienced) shall be accepted as evident.

In Merleau-Ponty this direction becomes more apparent so that he makes the claim that "perception is primary." This phenomenological "empiricism," now known as existential phenomenology, is one which attempts to understand all human behaviors upon the basis of or in relation to phenomenology of perception. Of course, the theory of perception which Merleau-Ponty developed was one in keeping with the reflective model I have described. It is the use of this model which differentiates his "empiricism" from its Anglo-American cousins. He

---

2. Merleau-Ponty, Maurice: "What is Phenomenology?" *Cross Currents*, Vol. IV, Winter 1956, p. 65.

rejected all sense-data theories and systems of causation as constructions rather than descriptions of perception and turned to a description which was closer to gestalt psychology and perspectivism as the basis for his understanding of perception.

I would note, however, that Merleau-Ponty's existentialism *is* this version of perceptualism. His use of phenomenological reduction is one which attempts to reach a level of pretheoretical experience, the experience of the (perceptual) lifeworld. He says, "By these words, the primacy of perception, we mean that the experience of perception is our presence at the moment when things, truths, values are constituted for us; that perception is a nascent *logos;* that it teaches us, outside all dogmatism, the true conditions of objectivity itself; that it summons us to the tasks of knowledge and action."[3]

This theory of evidence, regressive in its drive towards primitivity, remains in line with its Husserlian sense. To gain the perceptual lifeworld the suspension or critique of all merely taken for granted interpretations or presuppositions is to be undertaken. In this process Merleau-Ponty's arguments against the empiricists attack the doctrines of sensation as merely constructs which falsify primitive experience rather than explain it.

But, as Merleau-Ponty notes, the reduction is never complete because what it arrives at is always the essential assumption of being already in a world and it is this assumption which the phenomenologist wishes to explicate. The regressive direction of Merleau-Ponty's use of phenomenology nevertheless retains the bi-polar model which remains essential to its Husserlian understanding.

To this point, Merleau-Ponty may be seen as essentially phenomenological in his use of a basic model. What differentiates him from Husserl is in what he takes as the world and what it reflects as a subject. His "mirror" and his "eye" are distinguishable. The world, for Merleau-Ponty, is the perceived world. It is presumed to be concrete, expressive, and rich in its contents. It is also a "natural" world rather than the strictly bracketed world of Husserl's formal ontologies. In this sense Merleau-Ponty tends towards a realism more strongly than did Husserl.

The same pattern is repeated when the reflective turn is made. If the perceptual lifeworld is the object-correlate for Merleau-Ponty, one would

---

3. Merleau-Ponty: "The Primacy of Perception," *Existential Phenomenology* (Prentice-Hall), p. 41.

expect a symmetry in relation to the subject who must be thought of as a concrete perceiver. And this is the case. The problem of the body takes on a central role for the reflected side of existential phenomenology. The *embodied* or incarnate subject is the perceiving counterpart to the perceived world. *Le corps vécu,* usually translated as the lived body, is the perceiving subject in a perceptual world and the concrete finitude of the body corresponds to the perceived presence of the world. Merleau-Ponty retains the bi-polar Husserlian model, but interprets it through perception.

One could argue, however, that this extension of Husserl is legitimate and that existential phenomenology is but carrying on the program of the "late Husserl." But that is not quite the case. By the selection of a "perceptual mirror" Merleau-Ponty chose only a partial aspect of Husserlian intentionality as basic. The perceived world and the perceiving embodied subject selects as primary the experiential side of intentionality as its basis and tends toward making signification secondary.

This becomes more apparent when one examines Merleau-Ponty's view of language. Even if his theory of language never attained the degree of development that his theory of perception did, it remains the case that it embodies a direction which is necessitated by this perceptualist base. It is also the case that as he turned more and more to the problems of language that this perceptualism was called into question.[4]

At first the Pontean theory of language seems to parallel clearly his theory of perception. Just as perception begins with gestalts and unitary wholes, so the world is seen as primitively expressive. And just as the perceived world is always understood only in its relation to a subject, so is language considered only in relation to the existent speaking subject. In contrast to attempts to deal with language as if it were an empirical object, Merleau-Ponty insists that one begin with phenomenological speech.

But as this theory of language develops, a second meaning to Merleau-Ponty's phenomenological empiricism begins to emerge. His use of phenomenological reductions was one which always attempted to move back towards the perceptual lifeworld which at base becomes unspeakable. In return, speech becomes the counter-movement from the "silence" of the perceptual world to its expression in language. Thus Merleau-Ponty argues that language arises out of silence, out of gesture, and even that it

---

4. There is even some question about a possible hermeneutic direction in the late Merleau-Ponty, *cf. Le Visible et l'invisible.*

is metaphorically a kind of music. This theory of expression parallels the aim of a phenomenology of perception to a pre-theoretical world. The theory of expression is one which seeks a *pre-linguistic* basis for expression. Thus the whole weight of the Pontean theory of language concentrates upon the birth or coming-into-being of expression, the movement from silence to speech.

I shall not here try to show how this theory of language follows from certain aspects of phenomenological investigation nor make complaint of some of the problems which I believe Merleau-Ponty raises. But I would point out that it is because he takes the perceptualist base as primary that this theory of language follows.

Hermeneutic phenomenology as linguistic philosophy

But here I abruptly leave Merleau-Ponty, suspended as it were, and turn to the second main neo-Husserlian direction as it takes shape in the thought of Martin Heidegger. My interpretation parallels that which I used with Merleau-Ponty and continues the metaphor of the mirror. The mirror which Heidegger uses is the world of language in a broad conceptual and historical sense. And the side of intentionality which is developed is that which begins with problems of signification and meaning. Heidegger's presumptuous *fundamental ontology,* to my way of thinking, is a phenomenology of language. And it is from this phenomenology of language that Heidegger ultimately reads experience itself. This reading of Heidegger which sees him as hermeneut emphasizes aspects overlooked in interpretations which would make Heidegger an "existentialist."[5]

I begin by pointing up the frequent use of linguistic-historical metaphors in Heidegger's writing. For Heidegger, man is discourse (*Rede*); he is called (*Ruf*) to listen to the voice of Being; the famed destruction of the history of ontology is to be by means of a violent examination of philosophical language, etc. In his backward or regressive aim at phenomena, hermaneutics or interpretation becomes the vehicle to be used. Heidegger explicitly claims: "Our investigation itself will show that the meaning of phenomenological description as a method lies in *interpretation.* . . . The phenomenology of Dasein is a *hermeneutic* in the primor-

---

5. In certain respects, Heidegger is actually closer to a philosophic version of "symbolic interactionism" (Mead) than to existentialism.

dial signification of this word, where it designates this business of interpreting."[6]

The essentially linguistic or conceptual strategy is revelaed from the very beginnings of *Being and Time*. Instead of turning to Husserl or announcing in strictly Husserlian fashion a program and a method, Heidegger formulates his phenomenology by his own version and translation of Greek terms. The phenomenon becomes "to let that which shows itself to be seen from itself" (the manifest). And logos, again translated in Heidegger's sense, is *discourse* or language in a primary and broad sense.

But for Heidegger phenomena are mostly covered over, hidden, and the task of phenomenology is to let these phenomena appear. On closer reading, it becomes apparent that what covers over the phenomena is *the history of interpretation,* the way in which language is used. Thus to recover one's hearing of the voice of being one must loosen up and rework this covering. It is here that the long task of the "destruction of the history of ontology" begins and takes the long and varied detours via Kant, Descartes, Aristotle, and the pre-Socratics. Hermeneutics has as task the re-opening of language to its fundamental or "original" possibilities. For Heidegger the categories of thought we employ have become hardened and prevent us from seeing, or better, from hearing, what underlies our categories as basic phenomena.

The whole context of interpretation which appears therapeutic in some aspects as one which, through the distinctions of authenticity and inauthenticity, discourse and idle talk, seeks to uncover phenomena by hermeneutics. Heidegger wants us to "get back to" discourse, but to do so we must recognize and break through idle talk or mere abstraction. But what is important in this outline is to recognize that the way this is done is to take for the surrounding element which constitutes the world the element of language. It is from this recognition that we may understand the mirror Heidegger uses.

The functional outcome of choosing a linguistic mirror has more than one result. But it also changes the context of phenomenological questions. The substitution of a language world for a perceptual world moves what forms worldhood from the natural world to the cultural world. The field of human expression, the world of subjects. Secondly, the language world is one which re-locates the focus upon intersubjectivity from gesture to the fullness of language. Intersubjectivity here is the necessary

---

6. Heidegger, Martin: *Being and Time* (Harper & Row), pp. 61-62.

given from which one begins for there is no private language to be found.

Thirdly, one may expect to find, as Heidegger has already so well emphasized, that I am used by language as much as I am able to use language. But this is recognizable in the phenomenological context most precisely if one turns first to the language world as it gives itself out to be. One may expect to find that in certain respects, just as the concrete positionality of an embodied subject is constituted by the perceptual world, so will the hermeneutic subject be constituted by his language world and the task becomes one of specifying in what ways and to what extent this occurs. Secondly, one may expect to find that the subject changes and has a history in relation to the language world. We are already aware that subjectivity is differently understood today than it was at the birth of our culture and that the "self" of a child is quite different from that of the adult. There is a history to the subject just as there is a history to the culture. In fact, one may expect to find with this mirror, historical considerations playing ever stronger roles as the language world is noted in its subtle changes.

But thirdly, one may expect to find in a counter-fashion something about the way language (or thought, if you will) changes what is perceived. The world may be potentially expressive—but what it expresses is different for us than for others in certain respects. The reflective model applied to language has not yet been exhausted. All of this lies within the scope of Heideggerian hermeneutics. For my purposes here, however, it is sufficient merely to point up the differences in problems and directions implicit in the difference between existential and hermeneutic phenomenologies.

MIRRORS AND ONTOLOGIES

If the neo-Husserlians seem to take different "mirrors" from which the subject is reflected and if, as both seem to claim, what is arrived at is an ontology of human existence, it would seem we are back to a hall of mirrors. And although a series of mirrors may, by their very selections and exaggerations reveal possibilities previously unexpected, each remains partial and short of finality. It might seem that phenomenologists now must choose between existential and hermeneutic directions, between what is taken as basic: experience or language? immediacy or history? And it might seem at worst that this is a return to sheer metaphysics with resurrected, if modified, empiricists and idealists again dividing up.

I would suggest that this is not quite the case. And I return to a comment of Paul Ricoeur whose notions began this paper. Ricoeur argues that phenomenology of speech and a phenomenology of language are two quite different matters and focus upon quite different aspects of the whole linguistic phenomenon. And it is precisely this difference of task and focus of attention which holds the key to at least some of the differences between Merleau-Ponty and Heidegger.

By beginning with the "silence" of perceptual experience and by viewing language as expression, as the coming-into-being of significance. Merleau-Ponty in effect begins a phenomenology of speech. The subject struggling with language, to say the new, to express himself, is the focus of the perceptualist's immediacy. But by beginning with what has been said and by showing how we are used by our language and our interpretations, Heidegger begins with a phenomenology of language.

The phenomenology of speech and the phenomenology of language belong together. Immediacy without history is silent; history without speech is empty noise. And if the issues meet in a question of language, however differently that question is formulated on the Continent than in Anglo-American circles, it is not mere historical accident. The "linguistic turn" now belongs with the hedgehogs as well as to the foxes and the philosophy of language animates Paris today just as it does Oxford. And phenomenology through or in spite of its excursion through existentialism is returning full circle to Husserl. But this is a response to our time and I close with a comment by Ricoeur whose earlier comment suggested this line of interpretation.

> Today we seek a broad philosophy of language which would be able to account for the multiple functions of human signification and its mutual relations. How is language capable of such diverse usages as mathematics and myth, physics, and art? It is not by chance that we ask this question today. We are precisely the ones who use symbolic logic, exegetical science, anthropology and psychoanalysis, and who for perhaps the first time are capable of embracing as a unique question that of the reconstitution of human discourse. In effect the progress of the disciplines as disseparate as those mentioned have at the same time manifested and aggravated the dislocation of this discourse. The unity of human speech is a problem today.[7]

---

7. Ricoeur, Paul: *De l'Interpretation* (Editions du Seuil), pp. 13-14.

CHAPTER ELEVEN

Some Parallels between Analysis and Phenomenology

If one traces the history of the analytic philosophies in fairly broad expressionistic strokes rather than in pointillistic dots it appears that in certain ways that family of philosophies has more closely approached phenomenological insights than is generally noticed. And if one traces the history of phenomenological philosophy in the same size strokes it appears that language has become more and more a problem for it. This historical convergence can be seen in relation to certain views of the relation of language and experience.[1] In this paper I intend to first indicate what I take to be the movement of convergence and, secondly, show a certain parallelism between W. V. O. Quine and Paul Ricoeur in terms of their respective view of language and experience.

In the beginning a rather stark contrast appears between phenomenology and the analytic movement. This is particularly so if one compares the most extreme type of logical atomism with the phenomenological view. The key notions of logical atomism developed among the early analysts derive mainly from the work of Carnap, Russell, and the "early" Wittgenstein. Wittgenstein's *Tractatus*, which may be taken as representative, gives the clear impression that the world is composed of *atomic facts*, of discrete building blocks. These facts, given in sensory experience, are reflected in language. Discrete protocol sentences are the linguistic counterparts to the discrete atomic facts of which the world is

---

1. I use the term experience because it preserves a certain neutrality between phenomenologists and analysts. Let each interpret it according to their own philosophical filter.

built. Moreover, the more elementary, simple, and clear the sentence, the closer to the fact it could be. Knowledge (science) could thus be built from the bottom up by the addition of elementary sentences about facts if it is arranged in proper logical order.

If one suspends what may be called the *philosophical filter* of interpretation lurking behind this construction, i.e., that all atomic facts are basically sensory in nature and given according to a stimulus-response pattern, then it becomes possible to discern several important ideas contained in the early analytic view of language and experience. In the first place the assumption seems to be that the world is basically transparent and orderly in its construction. The ideal for philosophical language is one which seeks clear and distinct statements about the isolatable atoms of the world. If ambiguity or opacity is discovered it must either be excised or counted as false. Indeed, the tendency is to believe that any ambiguity or opacity is a problem of language itself rather than of the world. The major task of the philosopher is to remove this flaw by philosophic operation.

This conception of philosophy continues the rationalist ideal of clear and distinct ideas and also preserves the traditional sense that the philosopher is basically an ideal observer who is able, through his philosophical surgery, to arrive at "literal truth." Doing philosophy means dissolving problems through the clarification of language. This motivation remains strong even in the case to be discussed. W.V.O. Quine maintains his task is the "clearing of ontological slums."[2]

Thus in the instance of early analysis the relation of language experience is through clearly stated protocol sentences which express single facts. All systematic knowledge is built up from these foundations. To put it simply, factual sentences are the connection with experience; logic provides the framework of relations; and all other sentences are superfluous or meaningless so far as knowledge is concerned.

If one turns, in contrast, to early phenomenology it is not at all certain that linguistic problems are even major problems for the philosopher. And certainly the points of emphasis are quite distinct. For example, it appears that frequently a larger problem for the phenomenologist is the relation between the *speaker* and language. Speech as a

---

2. W.V. O. Quine, *Word and Object* (Cambridge: The Technology Press, 1960), p. 275.

type of intentional activity is more central.³ But as the phenomenologists began to investigate wider areas it became apparent that language does constitute a major problem.

Husserl's aphorism. "all subjectivity is intersubjectivity," has important linguistic implications.⁴ It is through language that subjectivity and the ways of intending objects attain intersubjective value.⁵ In later phenomenology the problem of language gains ground in several different ways. Heidegger introduces the notion of a hermeneutic, an exercise of philosophical clarification built upon meditations upon language itself in the hope of recovering the "pre-ontological" experience of Being. Mikel Dufrenne in *Language and Philosophy* traces language and its primary relation to experience to the poetic expressions of a first look at the world; he reaffirms J. G. Hamann's notion that "poetry is the mother tongue of the language."⁶ And Paul Ricoeur's reflective hermeneutic takes up the problem of language from within the richness of language.

If a phenomenological consensus about language exists it may appear like this: In contrast to atomism one might say that here the whole precedes the parts. Any meaning in the elements of language is to be found in relation to the whole of a given language. Language is not built up from discrete parts, but finds its significance in terms of indefinite possibilities within the living language.⁷ Moreover significance may dwell even within the silences, intersections, and intervals between the words. Again contrasting with logical atomism, the discrete statement is always bound to be incomplete and dependent upon a wider meaning in the language as a whole. It is also possible that so far as language reflects experience the ambiguous statement may also mirror something about the world and not be merely a confusion of language.

In summary: it is the totality of a living and constantly changing language with its many functions and many-layered structures which best reflects experience. Language may contain semi-autonomous bodies of

---

3. See the excellent summary of the matter in Merleau-Ponty, *Signs*, trans. R.C. McCleary (Evanston: Northwestern University Press, 1964), pp. 84-85.

4. Edmund Husserl, *Cartesian Meditations*, trans. Dorion Cairns (The Hague: Martius Nijhoff, 1960).

5. Quoted from Husserl's *Formal and Transcendental Logic* in Merleau-Ponty, *Signs*, p. 85.

6. J.G. Hamann, a contemporary of Immanuel Kant, is an often overlooked philosopher who asserted the primacy of language as a philosophical problem.

7. Merleau-Ponty, *Signs*, p. 42.

theory but they always remain at best incomplete and are but partial perspectives upon the world.

To stop at this point, however, would leave the two recent families of philosophy quite distant and unrelated. On the one hand we would have the early analysts doing a "logic of the sciences" based upon a type of reductive empiricism. And on the other hand we would have the phenomenologists doing a description of the many-layered structure of the world from their quite pluralistic view. But the story does not stop here. We now recognize two quite different directions in analytic philosophy.

The one side known as ordinary language philosophy may, in part, be traced to the "late" Wittgenstein. Wittgenstein evidently became less and less happy about his earlier statement of the problem and turned away from the atomism of the *Tractatus* to an interest in ordinary language. Evidently one of the problems became the complexity of the "facts." More flexibility was called for since language could not be simply reduced to protocol statements (nor the world to atomic facts). Wittgenstein indicated, "My propositions are elucidatory in this way: he who understands me finally recognizes them as senseless, when he has climbed out through them, on them, over them."[8]

What Wittgenstein came to believe, without ever abandoning his notion that the key to dissolving philosophic problems lay within the study of language, was that even an ideal language is no guarantee that one has adequately grasped the actual facts. An ideal language is no guarantee that what has taken as fact is so. Philosophy must become more a linguistic activity than ever if it is to discover the world aright.[9] Wittgenstein seems in some cases to have come to the conclusion that language itself is only a part of an activity which is at base nonlinguistic.[10] He seems to have come close to the phenomenological position regarding the need to describe this pretheoretical world when he indicates in the *Blue Book*, "I want to say here that it can never be our job to reduce anything to anything, or to explain anything. Philosophy really is 'purely descriptive.' (Think of such question as 'Are there sense data?' and ask: What method is there of determining this? Introspection?)"[11] Wittgenstein's following is also informative of certain parallels.

---

8. Wittgenstein quoted in W. Barrett and H. Aiken, *Philosophy in the Twentieth Century*, Vol. 2 (New York: Random House, 1962), p. 490.
9. *Ibid.*, p. 490.
10. *Ibid.*, p. 490.
11. *Ibid.*, p. 725.

With the scope of ordinary language philosophy Austin appears quite interesting. Austin, with most of the linguistic analysts, insists that language cannot be reduced to the three simple categories of statements (empirical, tautological, and meaningless) of the positivists. Rather there are many dimensions and functions within language—and presumably within experience. With Austin the philosophical task becomes one of pointing out the subtleties of language. Austin attacks many of the historic problems by first accusing traditional philosophers of being a bit too debate-minded. Had the traditional philosopher paid more attention to the richness and flexibility of ordinary language he might not have gotten himself into the dichotemous controversies (such as free-will versus determinism) which so often debilitate philosophical advance.

From the "late" Wittgenstein on one sees this movement away from rigidity and towards a more flexible view of language. In addition one sees the emergence of the notion that language reflects experience in a multitude of ways. This approach obviously has a greater affinity to the phenomenological sympathy for a recognition of multiple dimensions to the world and experience.

But my main concern is not with the ordinary language philosophers. It is rather with what I take to be a development from the positivist side of the family. In this country there appears to have been a wedding of certain positivist and pragmatic views which I think are resulting in still another parallel between analysis and phenomenology.[12]

It is with the work of W.V.O. Quine that one finds this direction stated in its boldest terms. Quine is perhaps best known for his "Two Dogmas of Empiricism" in which he attacks the distinction between synthetic and analytic statements held so dear by the early analytic thinkers. Quine's attack was waged on behalf of a different view of the realtion of language and experience. Quine puts the matter clearly:

> It has been the fashion in recent philosophy, both that of some of the English analysts and that of the logical positivists, to think of the terms of science and ordinary language as having some sort of hidden or implicit definitions which carry each such term back finally to terms relating to immediate experience. Now this view is clearly unrealistic. A better description, though countenancing the notion of immediate experience still, is as follows. On the one hand

---

12. James Edie has indicated that in certain respects William James approximates phenomenology.

> we have language, as an infinite totality of said or appropriately sayable phrases and sentences. On the other hand we have our sense experience, which by a process of psychological association or conditioned responses, is keyed in with the linguistic material at numerous and varied places. The linguistic material is an interlocked system which is tied here and there to experience; it is not a society separately established terms and statements, each with its separate empirical definition.[13]

Quine's statement of the problem indicates both his connection with the positivist version of analysis and his rather distinctive modification of that tradition. On the one hand Quine retains the same philosophical filter as the positivists. Wherever language does "key in" with experience it is primarily in terms of sensory experience interpreted behavioristically. These connections between language and experience Quine terms "surface irritations" appear upon the body of the language. And in some ways "surface irritations" appear to be quite like atomic facts—but not quite. Quine does insist that "occasion sentences," sentences which "command assent or dissent only if queried after an appropriate prompting stimulation,"[14] and "observation sentences" which are "occasion sentences whose stimulus meanings vary none under the influence of collateral information,"[15] are the closest to immediate experience.

But on the other hand, Quine's view of language seems to imply a strong rejection of logical atomism. The indefinite totality of language has what might be called a life of its own. It contains numerous interlocked systems and "bodies of theory" in addition to the most primary occasion and observation sentences. Thus if one wants to understand a term or a statement within the language this may be done only in relation to the wider linguistic connections.

What emerges in Quine's theory of language is what may be called a multiple-layered view of language and experience. The linguistic system is interlocked and connected in various (and often nonlogical) ways. And it is also layered. In short, a language is somewhat like a vast linguistic onion composed of many layers. Following this metaphor, the outermost layer is the one which "keys in" here and there with experience in terms of surface irritations. Here it is that one makes the primary statements

---

13. W.V.O. Quine, "On Mental Entities," *Proceedings of the American Academy of Arts and Sciences*, Vol. 80, No. 3, March, 1953, p. 198.
14. Quine, *Word and Object*, p. 36.
15. *Ibid.*, p. 42.

which Quine takes to be quite neutral or objective. He says, "Observation sentences peel nicely; their meanings, stimulus meanings, emerge absolute and free of residual verbal taint. Similarly for occasion sentences more generally, since the linguist can go native."[16] But the inner layers have less and less "experiential purity," i.e., the inner layers of the linguistic onion become more and more dependent upon larger bodies of theory. This is the case with all theoretical statements.

> Theoretical sentences such as 'neutrinos lack mass' or the law of entropy, or the constancy of the speed of light, are at the other extreme. It is of such sentences that Wittgenstein's dictum holds true: "Understanding a sentence means understanding a language." Such sentences, and countless ones that lie intermediate between the two extremes, lack linguistically neutral meaning.[17]

Here the picture emerges more clearly. At the surface there are more or less simple statements upon which agreement may be had; at the other extreme are the theoretical statements including philosophical ones. In between there are various connections and layers which span the gap, a rather great amount of linguistic onion skin.

The acceptance of this theory of language and experience in relation to philosophy has several results so far as Quine is concerned. In the first place it both relates philosophy to other types of theorizing and at the same time removes philosophy from any absolute position. The philosopher lives in the same linguistic world as anyone else and he must work his way around from within. This means that the philosopher cannot assume the "high and serene" balcony from which to observe the whole. The philosopher is within the maze; he is different from his peers only in terms of detail. Quine indicates:

> The philosopher's task differs from others' then, in detail; but in no such drastic way as those suppose who imagine for the philosopher a vantage point outside the conceptual scheme that he takes in charge. There is no such cosmic exile.... He can scrutinize and improve the system from within, appealing to coherence and simplicity; but this is the theoretician's method generally.[18]

In addition to this relativity the philosopher has one further difficulty. He stands, as it were, the farthest removed from immediate experience so

---

16. *Ibid.*, pp. 76-7.
17. *Ibid.*, pp. 275-6.
18. *Ibid.*, p. 276.

far as the layers of language are concerned. This means, Quine says, "No experiment may be expected to settle an ontological issue; but this is because such issues are connected with surface irritations in such multifarious ways, through such a maze of intervening theory."[19]

What, then, is the philosopher to do and how? The only help the philosopher-inside-the-onion has, according to Quine, is the device of "semantic ascent," that is, the philosopher shifts from talk about objects to talk about "objects" (words).[20] Or, if I may risk a paraphrase of this analytic version of the *epoché*, one may seek to discover something by refusing to talk in terms of literal truth, of belief, of the material mode, in short, of the natural perspective, and talk instead about words and the conceptual schemes.

The major task of the philosopher is to reflect upon language through language in the hopes of *clarifying* and *describing* areas of linguistic relationships which have heretofore been either muddled or misleading. But even this is done within the linguistic onion.

For Quine and, as I shall try to show, for Ricoeur, the border between language and experience is not a neat and clear one. Even the distinction between linguistic and non-linguistic phenomena, between words and their referents must be made linguistically. This *is* the hermeneutic problem.

In one sense Ricoeur (and much of recent phenomenology) begins where I have just left off with Quine. It is indeed the recognition of the hermaneutic problem which had led some phenomenologists more deeply into the problems of language. A favorite phenomenological distinction has been that between the pretheoretical world and the world as presented theoretically. There was Husserl's noematic-noetic correlation. There is the life-world and the reflections of thought upon that world. But at the same time all of these distinctions must be made *within* language. It may be true that linguistically we point to that which is non-linguistic but our pointing is in terms of a language.

Ricoeur deals with this problem as he struggles with his interpretation of man. In *La symbolique du mal* Ricoeur deals with man's understanding of himself and his situation in terms of the problem of evil. Ricoeur holds that the primary symbols and primitive myths of man hold a certain suggestive richness of thought which may be explored philosophi-

---

19. *Ibid.*, p. 276.
20. *Ibid.*, p. 272.

cally. That is, primary symbols and myths are expressions of man's self understanding; they are "words" which man pronounces upon himself. Philosophy, if it wishes to approach any kind of universality in relation to human experience, must reflect upon these issues and self-confessions (*l'aveu*).[21] It is in the light of this particular problem that Ricoeur raises the hermeneutic issues: "In contrast to philosophies concerned with starting points [we must begin] from within language and of meaning already there. [Philosophy's first problem] is not how to get started, but, from the midst of speech, to recollect itself."[22]

From the very outset one must be warned: Ricoeur's philosophical interest and also his philosophical filter are quite different from Quine's interests and filter. But this is not the focus of interest here. What is of interest is the great similarity, in structural terms, of the understanding of language and experience.

As Ricoeur orients himself "within language" it becomes apparent that he, too, accepts an "onion shaped" view of language and experience. In this case the place where language keys in with immediate experience is with various *primary symbols*. These are Ricoeur's counterparts to Quine's surface irritations. At the outset one must not ignore the quite different problem and filter. Where Quine is interested in logical theory, Ricoeur is interested in philosophical anthropology. Where surface irritations are linguistically neutral and express behaviorial occurrences primary symbols are opaquely suggestive and are filled with poetic richness.[23] So here the connection with experience is interpreted quite differently, i.e., the philosophical filter has a different mesh. But that is not the main point.

The main point is that for Ricoeur as for Quine there are certain privileged sentences or statements which afford a more direct connection between language and experience. (And who is to say at this preliminary stage that these connections may be or may not be of more than one type?) Both Ricoeur and Quine maintain a sense that at various points language does key in with experience.

But language does not key in with immediate experience at all points. With Ricoeur as with Quine, philosophy stands at a rather distant point

---

21. Paul Ricoeur, "The Hermeneutics of Symbols and Philosophic Reflection," *International Philosophical Quarterly*, Vol. II, May, 1962, p. 200.
22. *Ibid.*, p. 192.
23. *Ibid.*, p. 194.

from the primary statements. For Ricoeur philosophy is to be a *reflection* upon the symbols, its ultimate goal is to go beyond the symbol as such—though care must be taken not to distort the intentionality of the symbol.[24] Philosophy must remain informed by the primary statements, but its theorizing goes beyond them. As such philosophy stands the same risk that theory in general does for Quine. It remains within the system and it must recognize the need for correction.

Again, for Ricoeur as for Quine, between philosophy proper and the primary statements stands a maze of intervening interpretation or levels of expression. There is both interconnection, in which the philosophical task is the phenomenological job of understanding "symbol by symbol, by the totality of symbols,"[25] and there are levels of interpretation. In terms of Ricoeur's special problem there are primary symbols which are the most immediate responses of man's understanding of evil; then there are myths which are "first order spontaneous" interpretations of symbols; then there are theological doctrines which are third level interpretations, and so on. In brief, between philosophical reflection and primary statements stands a vast amount of intervening interpretation, many layers of onion.

How does the philosopher work through the layers? and what is his task? Again Ricoeur and Quine resemble one another. Ricoeur's version of "semantic ascent" is what he calls the *second naiveté* of a philosophical hermeneutic.[26] When the philosopher qua philosopher looks at symbols and myths he shifts from a material mode to a formal mode of understanding. That is, the philosopher is not interested in the "literal truth" which the believer may take the myth to hold. Rather the philosopher is already ascendant to the level of *interpretation*. He asks what is the intentionality of the myth apart from its cosmological scheme, apart from its logos. What is the theme of the myth? Ricoeur's own exposition of his hermeneutical theory is quite complex and need not detain us at this point. It is safe to say that when he examines given symbols and myths he does it more on the model of a sympathetic literary critic than that of the fundamentalist to the Bible. The point is simply this: in order to gain a philosophical perspective within language

---

24. *Ibid.*, p. 201.
25. *Ibid.*, p. 201.
26. *Ibid.*, p. 202.

the philosopher must ascend from the "literal" or material mode to the formal mode of interpretation. With this Ricoeur stands with Quine.

But the philosopher in his ascent must remain with his feet on the ground. He works out his problems within the fray rather than from above. Even philosophy cannot claim to be the concrete universal, says Ricoeur, since the philosopher cannot view the whole. The philosopher stands within a relativity of language and situation. His task is basically a descriptive and clarifying one. For Ricoeur this makes of philosophy basically a hermeneutic task, a process of reflection of language upon language in such a way that from within one may see the way from experience to theory.

Thus for Ricoeur from the phenomenological point of view, and Quine from the analytic, both recognize that language does key in with experience, but this connection is neither simple nor sure. One must always be wary in the sense that language may reflect as much upon language as it does upon experience. The philosophic problem is always, at least in one of its most important dimensions, hermeneutic or linguistic. In this I suspect both Ricoeur and Quine understand the significance of Neurath's aphorism:

> Wei Schiffer sind wir, die ihr Schiff auf offener See umbauen müssen, ohne jemals in einem Dock zerlegen und aus besten Betandteilen neu errichten zu könne.[27]

---

27. Quoted from Otto Neurath frontpiece to Quine, *Word and Object*.

CHAPTER TWELVE

Wittgenstein's "Phenomenological Reduction"

In recent years there has been a proliferation of studies and articles comparing the methods of linguistic analysis and phenomenology. Herbert Spiegelberg's " 'Linguistic Phenomenology' John L. Austin and Alexander Pfander,"[1] was among the early contributions to this literature. But until recently most such comparative studies have dealt with structural similarities and differences apart from historical connections. Paul Ricoeur's recent demonstration of the parallel internal developments of theory in Wittgenstein and Husserl from an early "abstract" to a latter "concrete" emphasis is a good example of possible parrallel evolution.

However, Spiegelberg's noteworthy sense of the historical and even personal connections between philosophers has raised a new set of questions. His article, "The Puzzle of Ludwig Wittgenstein's Phanomenologie (1929-?),"[2] suddenly reopened for me a question left dangling some years ago. I was struck when I first read the *Philosophical Investigations* by passages which seemed to be almost intimate arguments with husserlian phenomenology, but yet couched in emphases which seemed to fit all too neatly the curves of theories once more closely related. I had argued in class, but never in print, that there seemed to be some sort of "phenomenology" but with an inverted emphasis in Wittgenstein and

---

1. H. Spiegelberg, " 'Linguistic Phenomenology' John L. Austin and Alexander Pfänder," *Memorias del XIII Congreso de Filosofia, Communicationes Libres*, Vol. IX, pp. 509-517.

2. H. Spiegelberg, "The Puzzle of Ludwig Wittgenstein's *Phänomenologie* (1929-?)," *American Philosophical Quarterly*, Vol. 5, No. 4, October 1968, pp. 244-256.

at the same time I thought the key was to be found in Husserl's evaluation of imaginative variations in contrast to Wittgenstein's deliberate exclusion of them in favour of using concrete objects (bits of paper colored red, words on cards, etc.)

Spiegelberg's enticing discovery of a short-lived use of a generalized phenomenological vocabulary, presumably begin in 1929 just upon Wittgenstein's return to Cambridge, to its submergence at the latest in the 1933 *Bluebook* coupled to the hint of an anti-Husserl question suddenly jelled what had been missing in my earlier suspicions. And although I wish to be cautious and admit that the limited thesis argued here remains speculative and based upon the same limitations Spiegelberg suffered in having no access to unpublished Wittgenstein texts, I am now willing to offer a hypothesis: *Wittgenstein was influenced by a generalized phenomenological method which* provided in part a basis for the turn to ordinary language. *But at the same time the peculiar use of a "phenomenological reduction" takes a turn inverse to that of Husserl and towards the isolation and description of linguistic phenomena over a phenomenology of experience.* This hypothesis remains speculative to the degree that more comprehensive textual evidence is still wanting for more thorough confirmation of historical connections. But if the thesis does turn out to be plausible its potential challenge to the now "orthodox" interpretations of Wittgenstein, dominated by an "anglican" scorn for things European and by primarily neo-positivist empathies of North America, is worth the risk.

I have here chosen to open the question of a phenomenological reduction by way of the *Blue Book*. According to Spiegelberg's chronology and evidenced by the text, the phenomenological vocabulary as such has been submerged. But the investigations of Spiegelberg have provided clues about how and where this vocabulary leaves a trace of bubbles. There are some substantial textual hints. Two of these need initial note: (a) In the short period of its use, the term phenomenology is clearly linked to the increasing emergent use of grammar. A grammar, or phenomenology, is the descriptive laying out of structural possibilities of the phenomena in question: " 'Thus *phenomenology would be the grammar* for the description of those facts upon which physics erects its theories. . . . Is the theory of harmony at least in part *phenomenology, hence grammar?*"[3]

---

3. *Ibid.* [Spiegelberg's translations, italics mine], p. 254.

The *Blue Book* begins a study which frequently distinguishes a grammatical (hence phenomenological) study as one apart from both physics and psychology. Here, perhaps, lies one reason for the parallel set of problems Wittgenstein addresses himself to, problems which have been major themes in phenomenology as well: solipsism and privacy, a way between realism and idealism, a rejection of the cartesian tradition of mind and matter, etc.

(b) If grammar is a phenomenology its method must be essentially descriptive. This parallelism, often enough noted, must be more precisely developed. Phenomenologists point out over and over again that a descriptive method is one which seeks to avoid certain types of *reductive* (explanatory) tactics.[4] Rather than reduce all phenomena to some single basic substratum the task is to display the multiplicity and multi-dimensioned aspects of the phenomenon in question. The way to do this is to horizontalize (bracket out) the usual assumptions about the phenomenon. Wittgenstein in the *Philosophische Bemerkungen* points out that one must, in "inspecting the phenomena which we want to describe ... [try] to understand logical multiplicity,"[5] The *Blue Book*, and later the *Philosophical Investigations*, takes this even more rigorously. "I want to say here that it can never be our job to reduce anything to anything, or to explain anything. Philosophy really *is* 'purely descriptive.' "[6]

The grammatical, descriptive method which Wittgenstein begins to work out in the *Blue Book*, I shall argue here, is a submerged and inverted "phenomenological reduction" addressed to phenomena in such a way that *language* becomes the world-theme of this "phenomenology."

But it is now time to enter the problem from the bottom up. Grammars, essential structural characteristics of linguistic phenomena, are what we must understand. But first comes the question of how one arrives at the essences. I may pose this question in a hypothetical way:

---

4. There is a persistent confusion in this terminology. Reduction in the "bad" sense is used in phenomenological literature to mean a reduction to explanation whereas a phenomenological reduction is a reduction in the "good" sense as description.

5. *Ibid.*, p. 247.

6. Ludwig Wittgenstein, *The Blue Book*, Harper Torchbooks, 1958, p. 18. And if by grammar, Wittgenstein means phenomenology, here still in its earlier sense of a science of possibilities, then is it any wonder Moore can't understand what use Wittgenstein is making of "grammar"? Note Moore's perplexity in his report of Wittgenstein's lectures from 1930-33.

were Wittgenstein using some type of phenomenology what must the ingredients be? The answers from the argument for a viable parallelism with the suggested inversion at the point of reductions proper.

1. The first radical step of a phenomenology, *epoche*, functions as the conversion of a point of view. Whether epoche is understood as the bracketing of certain assumptions about the real existence of things, or the asserting of an initial set of systematic values which will create the focus of the method, or as a vehicle by which certain traditional or "natural" prejudices are to be overcome, the result is a change in perspective upon the phenomena in question. In Husserl's case all these aspects of epoche were directed against the "natural attitude" which was to be suspended and be replaced by a "phenomenological attitude."

Epoche, at one and the same time seeks to bracket the judgments which obscure the appearing of phenomena and opens the field of phenomena for description. In Husserl's case, however, this methodological device and an implicit metaphysical decision cross.[7] The field is understood (interpreted) to be the field of *transcendental experience* and thus from the first gives a weighted primacy to the question of the subject and his experiences.

But what if one employs the same method and applies it to a different set of questions? In this case the field to be inquired into, apparently at first more narrow, is the field of expressions. It is here that we find the Wittgenstein of the *Blue Book* and of the whole transitional period leading to the *Investigations*. The conversion of a point of view, "epoche," is quite systematically described. (I grant that more than a purely methodological question is involved here. Wittgenstein is obviously arguing with himself in relation to his earlier period and with Russell and Moore as well. But the later to be shown implications for a primacy of language over experience is too strong for me to believe these are the only figures in the debate.) What needs to be called into question is the long held traditional philosophic view of language. This linguistic "natural attitude," perhaps better termed the "logicist attitude," is what must be overturned and replaced with a descriptive or grammatical "attitude." I shall not here elaborate fully the constitution of a "logicist" prejudice which must be "bracketed" other than to indicate that it is at base precisely the tendency to view all expressions as if they contained or

---

7. See especially Ricoeur's critique in "Kant and Husserl," *Husserl*, Northwestern University Press, 1967.

were at bottom some kind of logic (or calculus as Wittgenstein puts it). A "logicist attitude" is from the start reductive in the bad sense as an explanation which lies behind or below the phenomena as they are actually "used."

To avoid this deeply held prejudice reductive assumptions must be purposely bracketed and replaced with a set of concepts in keeping with a descriptive approach. The *Blue Book* announces this program in its attempt to avoid what Wittgenstein calls "a craving for generality." He lists four aspects to this bracketing process which fall into two groups:

(a) The first group attacks what I am calling here the "logicist's attitude" which Wittgenstein wishes to avoid. There is a tendency, he claims, to look for a common property to all things included under a general term. But this is a first step in an exclusionary reduction. Instead, Wittgenstein proposes to use the concept of "family resemblances" in which likenesses may "overlap" without there being a common property throughout. Secondly, this tendency of craving generality is linked to what Wittgenstein calls our preoccupation with the methods of science which is throughout reductive in the sense of being an analysis which reduces everything to the smallest number of primitive laws and unifies them by means of generalization. This tendency must be staunchly resisted. It is "the real source of metaphysics, and leads the philosopher into complete darkness."[8] (Husserl and Heidegger locate the trouble at this point as well.) Rather, a careful study of particular cases should just as well reveal the complexities of grammar as the too easy generalization which overlooks this richness.

This first group of assumptions to be set aside, apart from the fact that some wittgensteinians seem not to have heeded the call to a non-reductive description, is less interesting than the second set of "logicist prejudices" which center on the role of experience and which open the way for the inversion of (husserlian) phenomenology. Wittgenstein strongly insists that in relation to general terms one must not suppose that there is a general mental picture which corresponds to the term. Like Berkeley, Wittgenstein holds that there can be no general idea *as an image* before the mind. But the reason for this, he claims, is the tendency to believe that "the meaning of a word is an image."[9] To so believe relates back to the deeply held notion that for every substantive

---

8. Wittgenstein, *Blue Book*, p. 18.
9. *Ibid.*, p. 9.

there must be an "object." The inversion to be introduced will attempt to show this is not the case.

In the case of meaning-as-image Wittgenstein may perhaps be seen to be arguing more with Empiricism than phenomenology and it does remain the case that a theory of experience much more clearly empiricist than phenomenological remains a ghost haunting Wittgenstein. But the attempt to bracket certain beliefs about experience goes farther in the second step of this group. Wittgenstein claims that there is a persistent "confusion between a mental state, meaning a state of a hypothetical mental mechanism, and a mental state meaning a state of consciousness (toothache, etc.)"[10] Here the swords will clash and the implied question is one which revolves around intentionality.

Spiegelberg notes that Wittgenstein does not seem to have utilized or grasped the implications of intentionality. To that may be added that Wittgenstein in no way seems to utilize a *reflective* method. Thus intentionality as a structure of consciousness without a reflective method must remain a "hypothetical mental mechanism" and will fall under Wittgenstein's version of "phenomenological reduction." I shall indicate below where intentionality does indeed function and give reason for its different placement by the absence of, or refusal to, accept a reflective method.

In short, Wittgenstein deliberately employs a conversion of a point of view to clear the field of expressions for descriptive investigation. The attempt to understand grammars remains in line with the earlier actual use of a phenomonological vocabulary in the *Philosophische Bemerkungen*.

But the transition to a descriptive stance is complex because there are at least two issues involved in Wittgenstein's own change of mind. The early Wittgenstein had sought for answers to his philosophical confusions in some form of ideal or artificial language. But in the transition which we see taking place from the *Bemurkungen* to the *Blue Book* it becomes apparent that the concept of primitive languages must change. A more modest goal of differentiating what is essential from what is not through the use of variational method becomes the goal. We begin to see the introduction of "free variations" to accomplish this task.

> As of now, phenomenological language or "primary language," as I have called it, does not appeal to me as a goal; now I no longer

---

10. *Ibid.*, p. 18.

consider it necessary. All that is possible and necessary is to separate what is essential to *our* language from its unessentials.

That is to say: if one describes, as it were, the class of languages which satisfy their purpose, then one has shown what is essential to them and thus *presented immediate experience immediately.* [Italics mine]

Each time I say that this or that presentation could also be replaced by this different one, we take another step toward the goal of seizing the essence of what is presented."[11]

Note preliminarily that the class of languages which satisfy their purposes—later to be designated as types of satisfactions in terms of different language games—*presents immediate experience immediately.* Experience will be read through expressions. In the later terminology of the *Blue Book* to have uncovered the grammar is to have thus presented experience. This point, extremely important for the inversion which occurs in Wittgenstein's use of a reduction, tends to give a weighted value to language over experience and eventually (but unsuccessfully in my opinion) to attempt to collapse experience into language.

Secondly, the variations by which the essential is to be described do not necessarily arrive at a pure primary language. By the time of the *Blue Book* a version of "inexact essences" has already appeared in the notions of concepts with "blurred edges" and "inexact usages."

But the radicalness of a wittgensteinian epoche remains transitional and the past still plagues Wittgenstein in the form of (a) an analytic version of preferring to build up the complex from the simple (as in the understanding of language games); (b) a narrow view of experience which remains limited to a largely Empiricist view; and (c) a lurking logicism which is never quite overcome.[12]

The change of goal, from primitivity as a possible ideal language to the primitivity of the essential, begins to take shape in the *Blue Book*. The specific use of a phenomenological vocabulary has disappeared but its trace remains. Compare this description of "language games" with the notions of PB:

---

11. Spiegelberg, *op. cite.*, p. 255.
12. Similar criticisms may be made of Husserl in relation to the problems which plagued his turn to phenomenology. There seems to exist an isomorphism between these two 20th century philosophies in the sense that the places within their theories where difficulties occur are functionally the same.

> I shall in the future again and again call your attention to what I shall call language games. These are ways of using signs simpler than those in which we use the signs in our highly complicated everyday language. Language games are the forms of language with which a child begins to make use of words. The study of language games is the study of *primitive forms of language or primitive languages.* [italics mine.][13]

Language games, to become the concept around which variations may be played, are the multivocal equivalents of the earlier univocal calculus of language.

"Epoche" as a conversion of a point of view in relation to a "logicist attitude" must be thoroughly rigorous in its rejection of any single hidden calculus of language. But beyond epoche lie the "phenomenological reductions."

2. The "reductions" employed by Wittgenstein *invert* the emphasis of husserlian phenomenology. Where Husserl reduced things to transcendental experience; Wittgenstein reduces things to linguistic usages—*the meaning is the use*. What must be seen here is that this "reduction" is one which wants to get back to the structures of language. This grammar must be displayed. Hence the "reductions" become the series of variations which successively uncover the grammar of expressions.

(a) The first step in the "reduction" is to remove the notion that words have necessary objects. In response to such questions as, "what is meaning?" Wittgenstein notes, "We are up against one of the great sources of philosophical bewilderment" a substantive makes us look for a thing that corresponds to it."[14] But for our purposes one way in which an "object" is supposed is of particular interest. (b) It is a case of supposing that some group of mental processes are the objects of meaning.

> It seems that there are *certain definite* mental processes bound up with the working of language, processes through which alone language can function. I mean the processes of understanding and meaning. . . . We are tempted to think that the action of language consists of two parts; an inorganic part, the handling signs, and an

---

13. Wittgenstein, *Blue Book*, p. 17.
14. *Ibid.*, p. 1.

organic part, which we may call understanding these signs, meaning them, interpreting them thinking."[15]

At just this point the phenomenologist may take heed. Is the "mental process" of which Wittgenstein speaks intentionality? And although I think it clear that the phenomenological sense of intentionality would undoubtedly be regarded a hypothesis regarding a mental process by Wittgenstein there seems to be lacking any clear concept of intentionality here at all. But its *function* does occur within language itself.

But a second look at what type of mental process Wittgenstein wishes to get rid of should also cause a second pause for the phenomenologist. Wittgenstein is clearly attacking what may be called a "cartesian" linguistic dualism. On the one side is a mechanical inorganic operation of signs; on the other an organic "soul" which understands. In rejecting this dualism Wittgenstein is asserting, perhaps inadvertently, that *there is no disembodied thought.*

(c) The exorcism of a disembodied mental process takes the shape of a series of ingenious free variations (mental experiments?). The first of these is one which brackets the imagination as an *imaging* ability. Wittgenstein suggests that we replace all mental images with concrete objects.

> "There is one way of avoiding at least partly the occult appearance of the processes of thinking, and it is, to replace in these processes any working of the imagination by acts of looking at real objects. . . . We could perfectly well . . . replace every process of imagining by a process of looking at an object or by painting, drawing, or modelling; and every process of speaking to oneself aloud or by writing."[16]

This *public* embodiment of the linguistic act is presumed to remove the mystery of the (private) image. "In fact, as soon as you think of replacing the mental image by, say, a painted one, and as soon as the image thereby loses it occult character, it ceases to seem to import any life to the sentence at all."[17]

Note here that while Wittgenstein nowhere denies that "mental processes" may in fact accompany thinking—which is now on its way towards being a type of linguistic performance—they are not *necessary* for mean-

---

15. *Ibid.,* p. 3.
16. *Ibid.,* p. 4.
17. *Ibid.,* p. 5.

ing. The variation has a quite narrow point to make: images are not necessary for meaning as such.

(d) Nor is thinking a translation of some pre-language into language. "The phrase 'to express an idea which is before our mind' suggests that what we are trying to express in words is already expressed only in a different language; that this expression is before our mind's eye; and that what we do is to translate from the mental into the verbal language." [18] But this is not this case, either, Wittgenstein argues. By a series of further exercises he hopes to show that thinking itself is a kind of linguistic performance. Note two of these: In the first we are asked to substitute any "thought" for its expression. "If you are puzzled about the nature of thought, belief, knowledge, and the like, substitute for the thought the expression of the thought, etc. The difficulty which lies in this substitution, and at the same time the whole point of it, is this: the expression of belief, thought, etc., is just a sentence."[19] Thinking, in the narrower sense which develops in the *Blue Book*, is a linguistic operation.

In the second set of variations the opposite side is tried. As a counter we are first asked whether we may speak without "thinking" in a kind of automatic behavior. The implied answer is yes. But then,

> "Speaking a sentence without thinking consists in switching on speech and switching off certain accompaniments of speech. Now ask yourself: Does thinking the sentence without speaking it consist in turning over the switch... that is: does thinking the sentence without speaking it now simply consist in keeping on what accompanied the words but leaving out the words? Try to think the thoughts of a sentence without the sentence and see whether this is what happens."[20]

The implied answer is clearly *no*.

What Wittgenstein is trying to show is the necessity of what I have called embodied thought. Thinking is at least a linguistic performance, an "operating with signs." Again, Wittgenstein does not deny that other mental accompaniments may be co-present with language, but he does want to establish the *primacy* of language in thought.

> I have been trying in all this to remove the temptation to think that there '*must* be' what is called a mental process of thinking, hoping,

---

18. *Ibid.*, p. 41.
19. *Ibid.*, p. 42.
20. *Ibid.*, p. 43.

wishing, believing, etc., *independent* of the process of expressing a thought, a hope, a wish, etc. [last italic mine] [21]

Rather thinking, the operation with signs, is the basic stratum to which may be affixed other mental occurrences.

[This variation] . . . rids us of the temptation to look for a peculiar act of thinking, independent of the act of expressing our thoughts, and stowed away in some peculiar medium. We are no longer prevented by the established forms of expression from recognizing that the experience of thinking *may* be just the experience of saying, or it may consist of this experience plus others which accompany it.[22]

For our purposes here the inversion is now complete. If linguistic performance (thinking now in the narrower of Wittgenstein's senses) is the base, then all the other accompaniments are related secondarily to the question of meaning. Embodied thought whether an "inner" or "outer" so far as any metaphysical solipsism would have it. Its results, oddly enough, are not too far from what could have been said by Merleau-Ponty as well: "We may say that thinking is essentially the activity of operating with signs. This activity is performed by the hand, when we think by writing; by the mouth and larynx, when we think by speaking. . ."[23] Only the vestige from a sense-data view of experience is excluded, "and if we think by imagining signs or pictures, I can give you no agency that thinks."[24]

Thinking is a concrete activity, operating with signs. All other experiences as accompaniements relate secondarily to language in operation so far as meaning is concerned. Thus in a way perhaps more literally than a Heidegger would put it, Wittgenstein intimates that "language speaks."

3. This leaves us with two dangling problems so far as any wittgensteinian "phenomenological reduction" is concerned. First, what happens to the notion of intentionality, the central structure of consciousness in the husserlian context? And secondly, what of the subject? The answer to both these questions is intimately tied to the total absence of a reflective method in Wittgenstein's thought.

---

21. *Ibid.*, p. 41.
22. *Ibid.*, p. 43.
23. *Ibid.*, p. 6.
24. *Ibid.*, p. 6.

For Husserl all structures of consciousness are not arrived at introspectively or directly, but reflectively and indirectly. The world of phenomena is first read on the object (noematically) prior to any description of necessary reflected structures (noetically). Intentionality is not first, but last in the order of progress. It is the goal of a phenomenology of experience.

But Wittgenstein from the beginning had another goal in mind, one which in many ways radically precisely brackets the fullness of experience. The goal is an understanding of *grammar*, the structure of language. An inversion, though, may retain a certain isomorphism with that form which it is inverted. I believe this is the case with Wittgenstein. Thus if the structure of language replaces the structure of experience in this "phenomenology" one can expect the *functions* of intentionality to be found *within language*.

And that is precisely the case. The "intentionality" of Wittgenstein is to be found in the concept, "the meaning is the use." The *life* of meaning is collapsed into language itself. The "meaning is the use" provides the structural key to all language. "But if we had to name anything which is the life of the sign, we should have to say that it was its *use.*"[25] This, whatever the size of the unit. "The sign (the sentence) gets its significance from the system of signs, from the language to which it belongs. Roughly: understanding a sentence means understanding a language."[26] To be able to correctly use a sentence implies the larger operation. "As a part of the system of language, one may say, the sentence has life."[27] Language, as it were, contains its own "life."

Further, the operations which Wittgenstein has in mind are of a particular type. They are immanent *within* language. He early distinguishes between "what one might call 'a process being *in accordance* with a rule,' and, 'a process involving a rule.'"[28] It is clear that it is the latter kind which are involved with meaning as use—"the symbol of the rule forms part of the calculation. . . . "A rule, so far as it interests us, does not act at a distance."[29]

All of this is understood by Wittgenstein as an *essential notion*

---

25. *Ibid.*, p. 4.
26. *Ibid.*, p. 5.
27. *Ibid.*, p. 5.
28. *Ibid.*, p. 13.
29. *Ibid.*, pp. 13-14.

regarding language. And here we reach one standard criticism of the wittgensteinian enterprise. While avoiding general concepts in the initial "epoche" as I have called it, Wittgenstein does employ one general concept, meaning as use. But in this interpretation its circularity with the original attack is not perfect. Instead, the generality here described, if understood as the linguistic correlate of intentionality, raises the level of the debate to what might be called a "linguistic ontology."

But is it an ontology with a subject? The answer must remain ambiguous in Wittgenstein's case. That there is no disembodied subject as a unique mental object is clear. And at points it appears that Wittgenstein is re-fighting the same battles fought earlier by Hume. But on the other hand there is a hint, already in the *Blue Book,* of what for a phenomenologist on the other side of the inversion sounds like making room for an implicit subject. But the implicit subject, even in answer to the question of "*who* operates with signs?" remains more "transcendental" than Husserl's ego. Nevertheless, Wittgenstein does produce some *grammatical* parallels to the "subject" and "object" concepts of the person. He notes, for example, that there are different cases of use involving "I," one of which is the use as "object," the other as "subject." In the case of "My arm is broken," "I have grown six inches," etc., possibilities of error, designation of a body or a particular person is involved. But in the "subject" use, "I think it will rain," "I have a toothache," etc., there is no provision for error—but this also implies that "To say, I have pain is no more a statement about a particular person than moaning is."[30] And here comes the particular rejection of any possible reflective procedure. Wittgenstein *denies* just what phenomenologists assert: "It would be wrong to say that when someone points to the sun with his hand, he is pointing both to the sun and himself because it is *he* who points..." But with a small reservation, "on the other hand, he may by pointing attract attention both to the sun and to himself."[31] What Wittgenstein calls attracting attention both to the sun and oneself is precisely what is referred to in a phenomenological reflexivity. I am known to myself—but via the otherness of the world and other egos because all subjectivity is already intersubjectivity. The turn to language ought, above all, to make this apparent.

---

30. *Ibid.,* p. 66.
31. *Ibid.,* p. 67.

CHAPTER THIRTEEN

Language and Experience

A problem for methods appears in a dialectic of phenomenology and linguistic analysis. This problem revolves around the *relation of experience to language*. I believe that in relation to this problem phenomenology and linguistic analysis display inverted models in which the countervalues of each method point to a naiveté area in its opposite.

In such a dialectic, however, a third consideration is presupposed, the working assumptions or hypotheses of the dialectic itself. I begin by stating these:

I am not sure that I know what language is. But I am relatively sure that proponents of linguistic analysis *think* that they know what language is and judge both phenomenology and the attempts to deal with experience upon this basis. I am not sure that I know what experience is either. But I am relatively sure that the proponents of phenomenology *think* that they know what experience is and judge language and analytic attempts to deal with language upon this basis.

Thesis #1: The methodological bases of phenomenology and linguistic analysis begin with inverse weightings of an essentially paired phenomenon, *language-experience*. The methodological drift of phenomenology is to begin with experience and attempt to deal with language from a description of experience in its movement toward expression. The methodological drift of linguistic analysis is, to begin with, a description of language and its structure from which experience is to be understood. These counterweightings are not neutral and lead to further consequences in relation to the paired experience-language phenomenon.

This thesis implies a further presupposition concerning the pairing of language and experience. Can one assume such a pairing? Although I shall not attempt to exhaustively justify this presupposition some support is called for. I find, when I am phenomenologically inclined (which is most of the time), that:

> Experientially I do not know what a prelinguistic experience is, since I already exist and am conscious in a world which is already immersed in language and one in which all my thinking is at least necessarily if not sufficiently linguistic in one of its forms. All my attempts to reach a total reduction to a prelinguistic world fail, and I cannot find such a "pure" experience.

And when I try to follow the analytic counter-method I find:

> Linguistically I do not know what a nonsubjective or nonexperienced expression is, since all speech acts occur in an experience-world which is a constant of my linguistic performances or is implied by all known linguistic formulations.

Thus the thesis which pairs experience and language may be stated both negatively and positively.

Thesis #2: There is no inexpressible experience. If there were, the implication would be an opting for *mysticism* in which the last word is silence but which is always belied by all forms of mysticism in the proliferous and indirect ways of describing silence. All silence may be described.

There is no expression without experience. If there were, the opposite of mysticism would be a crude *mechanism* in which the last word is the nonintentionality of a machine. Yet all machines are at least the indirect extensions of a very creative intentionality and experience, that of their inventors and programmers. If these persons prefer to model their minds upon their embodied constructs and ignore their prior "God role," they should not belie what comes first in the order of being both logically and chronologically. Positively: *Language and experience must be dealt with together as the paired foci of the single ellipse of subjectivity.*

DIALECTICS: THE INVERSION OF METHODS

The first moment of a dialectical movement toward the understanding of language and experience is one which locates limits to the theories which deal with the two foci of this paired phenomenon.

Phenomenology as a theory of experience: The phenomenological claim, "to the things themselves," is a theory of evidence in which the weighting of evidence finds its fulfillment in (immediate) experience and more particularly, in the late Husserl and much so-called existential phenomenology, in perception. Even if this immediacy is arrived at reflectively and thys indirectly rather than by simply introspection, the goal of phenomenology remains a pretheoretical and basically perceptual world. To secure this evidence the whole of the epoche and the phenomenological reductions are used to remove all factors which would obscure the richness of that experience.

The method is thus regressive in its direction, and attempts, layer by layer, to remove the secondary or tertiary series of presuppositions or beliefs which cover over or distort the original phenomena of pretheoretical experience. The suspension of the "natural attitude," the overcoming of abstractions and constructionist reifications, etc., all fall in this process of removal which successively reveals the naivetés and errors involved in taking theoretical constructs for experience itself. If experience is to be described in its richness, such a reduction of presuppositions, but not of experience, is necessary.

But such a method involves a circle which may be shown by an ambiguity which covers the idea of experience. In a broad sense, not only the basic perceptual life-world is experience, but the very presence of the theories, reified or not, constitutes part of experience. In this context phenomenology as a theory is itself the circle of experience within experience and its reductions are the arranging and valuing of how this global situation is to be understood. Within the circle of experience relative values are placed upon what is basic (the life-world or perception) and what is secondary (constructions).

This internal weighting of experience in relation to experience creates an effect in relation to language. With the primary weight upon a pretheoretical experience, language becomes secondary and is understood as a mediating function. In relation to language, the pretheoretical experience is termed prelinguistic, and phenomenology concentrates upon the movement from experience to expression. Language is understood to mediate experience.

The circularity of experience with experience within phenomenology is a recognition of a fate common to all theories and in itself is to be taken neither as a negative nor as a destructive criticism concerning the productivity of phenomenology. But by beginning from this internal circularity of experience with experience, the implication for language may be better understood. The implication is one which not only makes language secondary to experience but also tends to allow phenomenology to assume certain language functions. The way in which this effect occurs may be indicated in two examples:

Beginning students in phenomenology usually undergo what may be characterized as a sense of discovery. When they first begin to operate phenomenology as a philosophical method and attempt to describe their own experience phenomenologically, they are often struck by the complexity and richness of those experiences. But equally interesting are the linguistic effects of this operation in terms of what may be described as a *struggle with language*. Almost without exception the student reports variations of an "I-mean-more-than-I-can-say" phenomenon. And through the struggle with language the student begins to weave metaphorical statements, create neologisms, or even turn to quasi-poetic or literary forms to describe the newly discovered fullness of experience.

Nor is this discovery limited to students, since what they do is a repetition of what often occurred earlier in the work of the masters. Need I point to the predominance of newly coined terms and words which have emerged in phenomenological literature, which, save for their familiarity to us now, must appear clumsy: "being-in-the-world," "owned" or "lived" body, "incarnation," etc.? And the well-known turn of particularly existential phenomenologists to literary forms is not without reason.

I am implying that the very weight of (immediate) experience in phenomenological theory makes this a first operational outcome. But this outcome affects the phenomenological theory of language as well.

When one turns to the phenomenological literature on language, it turns out that most of it is a phenomenology of speech or of expressing. The emphasis is placed upon the genesis of an expression as it arises from the "prelinguistic" experiential basis (variously thought of as gesture. Merleau-Ponty; silence, Heidegger; or poetic symbol, Ricoeur). This emphasis is not accidental but a result of what the theory weights from the beginning. It is the intention to signify, the struggle with bringing experience to expression, the *vouloir-dire* of the speaking subject which seems to take precedence. The first move of a phenomenology of language is modeled upon its theory of experience.

Again, I do not wish to disparage this attempt—in fact, I praise it insofar as the phenomenological rediscovery of the richness of experience is a gain over the usually sparse or constructed notions of experience found in empiricist and most nonphenomenological accounts. But at the same time the selective weighting of experience over expression creates a naiveté area in phenomenological vision.

This limitation is most dramatically pointed up when the inverse method of linguistic analysis is placed dialectically up against a phenomenology of expression. (Note in passing that an inversion may indicate the opposite side of a single phenomenon so far as method is concerned.) This counter-weighting in linguistic analysis may be displayed in reverse order by noticing that the phenomena which tend to take precedence in analysis belong to the class of "I-don't-know-what-I-mean-until-it's-said" phenomena.

First, examples: If I undertake to write a book or an article I sometimes find something unusual going on. I make a decision about what is important and attempt to follow out the thought, only to find that the thought has a "life of its own," a "logic," which appears to me. This becomes more dramatic if, on the following day, I undertake to vary the decision even slightly and I find it necessary to almost totally revise what I had previously written. Experienced persons know very well that it is dangerous to attempt revisions and that to change a paragraph may mean to change a book. Need I point to the furious arguments which occur over differences in first as against second editions? It is a language phenomenon of this type which may be seen behind Wittgenstein's "Roughly, understanding a sentence means understanding a language."[1]

To get at these phenomena the linguistic analyst creates a different weighting of evidence. He suspends or suppresses immediate experience and plunges into a circle of language, the analysis of language by means of a second use of language. This circle which weights first or ordinary uses as prior to analytic or secondary uses is a counter-reduction compared to phenomenology. Austin says, "Ordinary language is *not* the last word: in principle it can everywhere be supplemented and improved upon and superseded. Only remember, it is the *first* word."[2] From his point of view, experience, which becomes secondary, is structured via

---

1. L. Wittgenstein, *Bluebook in Philosophy in the Twentieth Century*, Vol. II, New York, 1962, 714.
2. J. Austin, "A Plea for Excuses" in *Classics of Analytic Philosophy*, New York, 1965, p. 386.

language. Through the increased sensitivity to the "logics" and complexities of language he better understands experience. Again Austin: "When we examine what we should say when, what words we should use in what situations, we are looking again not *merely* at words ... but also at the realities we use words to talk about: we are using a sharpened awareness of words to sharpen our perception of, though not as the final arbiter of, the phenomena."[3]

Thus the struggle which emerges is a struggle with the complexities of languate through which a sharpened awareness of the structuring of experience may be had. In the process the linguistic inversion finds the other side of the experience-language phenomenon to reveal the same investigatory excitement originally noted with students of phenomenology.

As the analyst looks at language he discovers a previously unnoted wealth and complexity. "But I owe it to the subject to say, that it has long afforded me what philosophy is so often thought, and made, barren of—the fun of discovery, the pleasures of co-operation, and the satisfaction of reaching agreement."[4] Language is discovered with an unexpected fullness which continues to point up the "I-don't-know-what-I-mean-until-it's-said" phenomenon.

The analyst is finally led to allow his own "bracketing" to remain in effect and to see the turn to language as the structuring of even the most complex experiences. Language, as experience, is rich so that, as Austin indicates,

> ... the distinctions embodied in our vast and, for the most part, relatively ancient stock of ordinary words are neither few nor always very obvious, and almost never just arbitrary; that in any case, before indulging in any tampering on our own account, we need to find out what it is that we have to deal with; and that tampering with words in what we take to be one little corner of the field is always *liable* to have unforeseen repercussions in the adjoining territory.[5]

The second use of language in analysis finds the same difficulty which the phenomenologist finds. The struggle to describe language leads to "performatives," "behabitives," "illocutions," etc. As a field the world

---

3. *Ibid.*, p. 384.
4. *Ibid.*, p. 379.
5. J. Austin, *Sense and Sensibiliia*, New York, 1964, p. 63.

of language evidently displays parallel problems to what the phenomenologists call experience. In short, the analytic turn to the richness and strength of language, particularly in its directive or structuring power, is already a latent "phenomenology" of language as contrasted with a phenomenology of expressing. The linguistic-analytic reversed reading of the language-experience phenomenon allows this to stand out.

The choices of phenomenology and linguistic analysis remain inverted to the extent that different phenomena are developed in relation to the different weightings of the language-experience phenomenon. But both must be re-joined for a philosophical understanding of language and experience.

Where, then, does a dialectic of inverted methods lead? For me, back to the initial hypothesis concerning a need to maintain that language and experience are paired phenomena. I could suggest that even the minimal alternation of a phenomenology of expression with the analysis of ordinary language leads somewhere. The student of phenomenology who finds difficulty in his struggle to give birth to language would do well to take Austin's advice and turn to the dictionary, to legal distinctions, to psychology, and—I would add—to literature. There he would find an already extant wealth often unsuspected by the philosopher. Counterwise I probably need not mention that the inverse side of this investigation is the analyst's need to look again to the experience of expressing and referring itself if he wishes to understand the why of linguistic wealth.

So my argument makes its own circle, and the end is the beginning which wants to presuppose that language and experience are paired. But it is a beginning in another sense, a beginning which is in keeping with a return to the early Husserl. H—as Paul Ricoeur points out, "In Husserl's first works ... consciousness is defined not by perception, that is to say by its very presence to things, but rather by its distance and its absence. This distance and this absence are the power of signifying, of meaning .... Thus consciousness is doubly intentional, in the first instance by virtue of being an intuitive fulfilling. In short, in the first works, consciousness is at once speech and perception"[6]—then in my terms, subjectivity is always at once language *and* experience.

---

6. P. Ricoeur, *Husserl: An Analysis of His Phenomenology*, Evanston, Illinois, 1967, p. 204.

CHAPTER FOURTEEN

Singing the World...

Phenomenology is a revolution in man's understanding of himself and his world. But the newness and radicality of this revolution is faced with a problem, the same problem which arises in the epiphany of any new phenomenon. What phenomenology has to say must be made understandable—but what it has to say is such that it cannot be said easily in a language already sedimented and accommodated to a perspective quite different from that taken by the revolutionary. What eventually may be said must first be "sung." One only gradually learns to hear what sounds forth from the "song."

Not long ago an illustrative event of like dimensions occurred when the "songs" of whales were recorded. The listener, in every case known to me, would first be taken aback by the strangeness, the mysterious, enchanting uncanny quality of the "songs." Fascinated and even awed by this new "language" from the sea, deep stirrings of feelings occurred. Then a second phase of appropriation would begin through associations and metaphors: "That's *like* a bull bellowing," "It's *like* electronic music," "2001," "Now I can see how the legends of the sirens began." Here the listener attempts to relate the uncanny to something which is already familiar—and that's as far as most go. With the mysterious partly domesticated one is satisfied. But a further thought is possible: this is, after all, neither siren, nor electronic music, nor bull—it *is* the humpback whale sounding forth, "singing the world" in his own way. It is for us to listen, to enter that strange song as best as we can if we are to discern the contours of that world. For this, more than curiosity is called for. The whalesong issues a call to those whose resonances we cannot yet fully respond.

Language, "singing the world," is a philosophical problem. But that problem is more acute for the phenomenologist. The phenomenologist, faced with ordinary language filled with the sediments of a past history, must learn to sing in a new way. Merleau-Ponty was quite aware of the difficulties of both saying and hearing something new in his struggle to express himself. Of philosophies he said, "I begin to understand a philosophy by feeling my way into its existential manner, by reproducing the tone and accent of the philosopher. In fact, every language conveys its own teaching and carries its meaning into the listener's mind" (PP, 179).

I want to pose the question of language as the foreground focus in this essay on Merleau-Ponty because language is one, if not *the* archimendian point from which other questions may be levered from their background dominance. Behind, under, eventually beyond spoken language lies the world of perceived, wild being which is Merleau-Ponty's more apparent focus. For him it is through the question of perception that the question of language and expression is reached—but it is through the question of language that the enigmas of perception may also be seen.

Nor are the question of language and perception separable for Merleau-Ponty. Phenomenologically the world is already primitively given as meaningful in some sense. There is no pure datum, no raw qualia or pure sense from which to begin—rather man begins immersed in a world already significant, already both "natural" and "cultural" and the phenomena of immersion are the first to be interrogated. Thus if I begin by reversing Merleau-Ponty's emphasis it is because that reversal is suggested by his work itself. Insofar as perception and expression remain paired it is possible to begin from either side of the pairing, noting of course, that a reversal of order may also reveal aspects not apparent from the other side.

The initial practical problem—how does one make phenomenology understandable?—is at base more profoundly philosophical. It is too easy for the philosopher already assuming and inhabiting the "phenomenological attitude" to hold that the problem is not one of language at all. Nor is it, if all problems of language are those of particular propositions or of logics or grammars. The problem is one of a shift in stance. Once one learns to "see" as a phenomenologist, then what has been said by Husserl, Heidegger, and Merleau-Ponty appears neither obscure nor ambiguous. The problem is one of attaining a perspective, not one of uttering a correct formula. But this shift of perspective *is* a problem of language in a deeper sense. In elaborating the non-neutral, embodied theory of language in the *Phenomenology of Perception*, Merleau-Ponty noted that language "presents or rather it *is* the subject's taking up of a position in the world of his meanings." (PP, 193)

In this preliminary sense phenomenology, too, is the taking up of a position in the world of philosophical meanings. It, too, "sings the world" in its own style. And our task is to listen to that "song."

MERLEAU-PONTY'S EMERGENT THEORY OF LANGUAGE

I shall attempt first to develop some of the characteristic marks of Merleau-Ponty's notion of language. By situating his work in the context of a philosophical tradition and noting some features of the growth of a radical language, by outlining the distinctive features of an explicit theory of language, and then by noting the role language plays vis-a-vis perception, I hope to show the justification for this reversal of emphases.

A. *Strategy*

In the preface to the central book, *Phenomenology of Perception*, Merleau-Ponty explicitly situates his work in the context of the phenomenological philosophy issued earlier from Husserl. Merleau-Ponty sees his own development of phenomenology as a nuanced divergence from certain aspects of husserlianism. First, the perceptual world is primary, the base from which one must begin and the primitive field which must be thoroughly explored. Second, the examination of this field will yield certain essential ambiguities about man and his relations to his world which are revealed better by a focus upon the *genesis* of meaning than by attaining a description of stable essences. And, third, the genetic emphasis will result in the development of an *existential* as contrasted with a transcendental idealist philosophy.

In situating himself alongside Husserl, Merleau-Ponty also adapts and refines a strategy used earlier by Husserl. *Phenomenology of Perception* employs a polemic against both empiricist and rationalist traditions, against their mechanist and intellectualist outcomes. Posed positively against these traditions is the emergent existentialist philosophy developed by Merleau-Ponty. This positive position belongs to that class of contemporary "anti-cartesian" philosophies which reject the dualism of (mechanical, material) extended substance and (psychological, subjective) mental substance.[1] In contrast, Merleau-Ponty's existential position elaborates a unitary theory of embodied being.

But taking a polemic position is taking a position within an already constituted world of philosophical meanings. There is a price to be paid: not only must the existentialist position which emerges be drawn in contrast to the dominant philosophies, it must also first address itself to its opponents in the very language of those opponents. If "cartesianism" is to be rejected, what replaces it? If sense data are rejected, what is perception? The form of the question resituates us in the midst of a linguistic, expressive problem. If there is to be a new framework and a new language to express the insights appropriate to an existential phenomenological position how are those expressions to emerge from the non-neutral philosophical past?

Three degrees of increasingly radical language uses are discernible: (a) one seeks to use standard terms and gradually change their meanings, one adapts them to new usages. (b) One creates new terms (neologisms, compound words) and employs metaphors to infuse new meaning. (c) And one borrows words from other contexts not previously used by philosophers. (One might add that the result (d) would be an extension in which the new language will be a new technical vocabulary as the new tradition itself begins to re-sediment after the stirring it initially caused.)

Merleau-Ponty utilizes all three of these levels, but in varying stages. (a) Early the tendency is to be more conservative. *The Structure of Behavior* attempts to infuse gestalt germinology with a nascent phenomenology. Within the polemic structure of *The Phenomenology of Perception* the standard terms are again re-worked. Indeed, key philosophical terms are often dealt with in the manner of (a) refilled with new meaning. "Perception" is a significant sample. Perception is primary for Merleau-Ponty, but perception becomes both broader and more inclusive than its previous philosophical use. His defense of the thesis of the primacy of perception before the Societe Francaise de Philosophie is an attempt to widen the very meaning of perception.

> By these words, 'the primacy of perception,' we mean that the experience of perception is our presence at the moment when

---

1. Two things are worth note here: Certain forms of contemporary philosophies, particularly some linguistic analysis, have revolted against "cartesianism" in forms other than phenomenology. Secondly, "Cartesianism" is to be taken in its popular cultural sense rather than as a direct reading of Descartes.

things, truths, values are constituted for us; that perception is a nascent logos; that it teaches us, outside dogmatism, the true conditions of objectivity itself; that it summons us to the tasks of knowledge and action. (EP, 41)

Here "perception" must carry a load seldom imposed upon it by philosophy since its equivalent in the presocratics.

Similar adaptions and transformations happen with "subject," "thinking," "imagination," "object." But the essentially conservative strategy of importing new meanings to old terms is surpassed by (b) the introduction of increasingly suggestive coined terms and metaphorical uses. Already begun by Husserl and Heidegger, Merleau-Ponty accepts and expands the vocabulary of newly coined terms, "lifeword," "being-in-the-world," "intersubjectivity," "lived body," and to these adds a series of at least metaphorical uses of "silence," "incarnation," "gestural meaning," "singing the world."

The coined terms are quasi-technical from the beginning, despite their odd ring to the uninitiated. "Lived body" (*corps vécu*), for example, is meant both to contrast with the objectified sense of body used in the sciences and to refer to a primary, non-reduced sense of living being as embodied being. Similarly, "intersubjectivity" is meant to contrast with the subjective state of private selves and to positively suggest that we are already "outside ourselves in the world."

Even as technical terms much of their strength comes from evocations not found in the traditional and key terms of (a). This evocative sense is stronger yet in the metaphorical uses. The "silence" which precedes and which indirectly conveys meaning within speech, "singing the world" which precedes the philosophical norm of conceptualized meaning, pushes us further towards a radical and different philosophical vocabulary.

(c) Although there is a continuum of radicality from metaphor to the importation of words from spheres not previously used by philosophers, to my mind the most radical and interesting use of language comes into greater prominence with Merleau-Ponty's later writing. *The Visible and the Invisible,* itself an evocation and suggestive title, brings us "flesh," "chiasm," "intertwining," "perceptual faith," and "wild being." This is "wild language" more akin to a literary genre than to much philosophy. Merleau-Ponty's struggle with language leads him beyond the strategy of transforming terms to the initiation of a radical discourse.

What we are seeing here can be stated quite simply although the reality which is embodied in this development of language is far from simple. Simply, as the implications of the phenomenological revolution become more clear the more radical the use of language becomes. The new wine threatens to burst the older philosophical wineskin of terms. We are witnessing a birth of philosophical meaning. This is the case even if we must allow that the rent of the wineskin may eventuate in the dissolution of philosophy as it was previously known—that, at least, is one possibility.

The emphasis within Merleau-Ponty's theory of language upon the genesis of meaning is thus both a result of the demands of the phenomenological turn *and* a reflection upon Merleau-Ponty's own philosophical experience.

B. *The Theory of Language Mirrored after the Theory of Perception*

The "anti-cartesian" polemic of *The Phenomenology of Perception* forms the background against which both the emergent theories of perception and expression take shape. The argument which rejects both empiricist and intellectualist interpretations of perception and speech is one which attacks any notion of dualistic "purity." Both traditional interpretations maintain a *pure* (psychological) mental being and a *pure* (mechanical) material being. In contrast, the existential theory, based upon a phenomenological interrogation of experience, claims that such purity is constructed, not found.

Rejected are all notions of pure data, sensory or conceptual. Accepted is an essential ambiguity of the perceptual object, an incompleteness, and openness to multiple possibilities, all of which Merleau-Ponty argues is true to the actual perceptual experience. Rejected are both the objective (mechanical) body and the inhabiting clear thinking, transparent intelligence (mind) as immediate interpretations of experience. Accepted is the embodied subject whose every action is subject to an initial movement from the uniformed to the formed, whose gesture precedes any later attained clarity of intellection. Rejected is an objectively given world whose reality is merely to be discovered (constructed) by the right method of formal geometricization. Accepted is a world which is always pregnant with significance, but whose meaning must be re-won through an interrogation of its presence. The lifeworld appears between the subject and the world within the focus of perception.

The outcome of this line of thought on a functional level is to recognize that any theory of the body is already a theory of perception and, inversely, that any theory of perception is already a theory of the body. Thus the complete overthrow of both versions of "cartesianism," empiricism and intellectualism, is implied. The outcome on the ontological level is the rejection of the psycho-physical dualism which pervades the sciences of man, and the affirmation of an existential ontology of embodiment as the root source from which any adequate theory of body and perception must arise.[2]

The lived body, the embodied subject immersed in a world pregnant with unwon significance becomes the basic theme of the existential version of the primary perceptual situation. This unitary and relational ontology is held to transcend the dualism of "cartesianism."[3]

The theory of expression, in *Phenomenology of Perception*, is situated within the patterned after and upon the theory of perception. It follows the same polemic pattern vis-a-vis the "cartesianism" of dominant linguistic theory that the theory of perception follows in relation to psycho-physical dualism. This is the "cartesianism" which makes language psycho-physical. (Physical) *sounds*, in the case of speech, are the pure body-matter-extension of language, while (psychological) *meanings* are the mind of language. These two separate and distinct realms of linguistic beings are "related" in some way in actual language.

While it is important to see how the "cartesianism" of the linguistic sciences is isomorphic with that of other forms of psycho-physical

---

2. Merleau-Ponty remains ambiguous in relation to a reconstruction or an overthrow of science as presently constituted. On one hand he affirms the essentially husserlian reformism towards science—the task of phenomenology is to "measure the distance between our experience and this science" (EP, 44)—which would leave science as a discipline *interpreted* by phenomenology. On the other there is the tendency to radicalize ontology through "wild meaning" (VI, 155) which would seem to imply a different direction entirely.

3. Note here that the existential position being developed remains dependent upon "cartesian" terminology. The dualism is transcended in concept and intention, but not clearly in expression.

4. The linguistic sciences thus are divided into realms very like those of physics and psychology in relation to the body and perception. Formal, axiomatic, mathematical linguistics—the "physics" of language—deal with abstract relations: semiotics. Language, here, is idealized and objectified and the subject is "bracketed out." Language is viewed as like a machine. Semantics, as in all "cartesianism," which attempts to reintroduce the subject, remains primitive and at a distance from the successes of formalized linguistics. Moreover, I suspect that the various schools of linguistics are open to interpretations which parallel the four logical alternatives to body-mind relations (materialism, idealism, interactionism, occasionalism).

dualism, it is more important here to begin to discern the existentialist alternative concerning language posed by Merleau-Ponty. This alternative again parallels what was done with the theory of the body and perception. Language, expression, is ontologically always found *embodied*. "The word has a meaning." (PP, 177) Merleau-Ponty's whole theory of language is one of embodiment.

The argument is essentially the same as that used for the lived body—the concrete experience of speech and language is always first and primordially one of embodied meaning. A pure sound without significance is a construct (phonemes, morphemes, etc., are conceptual "explanations" of sounds)—they do not occur within concrete experience. But so is a pure thought! Both are the linguistic equivalents of sense data, the object body, and mental activity of the empiricist and intellectualist interpretations. They are constructions which "explain" the ambiguities of experience. Linguistic "mechanics" on one side and pure "intelligence" which merely uses language as a tool on the other both fall short of nothing concrete incarnation of meaning which Merleau-Ponty offers as the existential alternative.

"The word has a meaning," is the linguistic equivalent to the embodied subject. "The meaning of words must finally be induced by the words themselves . . . immanent in speech." (PP, 179) Existent language is embodied expression while both a pre-significant sound and a post-linguistic thought are dualistic constructions. Embodied expressive meaning thus parallels the embodied perceiving subject.

This theory of embodied meaning is, I believe, the central focus around which the usually noted features of Merleau-Ponty's language theory radiates. Both (1) the "return to the speaking subject" and (2) the "primacy of speech" usually remarked upon by commentators are dependent in their significance upon the central notion of embodied meaning.[5]

Furthermore, what must be seen as inextricably tied to the key of

---

5. See especially Paul Ricoeur, "New Developments in Phenomenology in France: The Phenomenology of Language," *Social Research*, Vol. 34, no. 1, 1967. Ricoeur quite correctly notes the primacy of the subject and speech as the necessary focus of Merleau-Ponty's existentialism. He is further correct in seeing that the ultimate implication leaves out a connection with modern linguistics (p. 11). But he apparently does not see that the question of language which transcends *me* is included in Merleau-Ponty's question. The question of "silence" is not merely related to a phenomenology of speech in contrast to a phenomenology of language.

embodied meaning is the method of phenomenological genesis which Merleau-Ponty sees as his nuanced divergence from Husserl. The phenomenology of genesis is what creates the full *existentiality* of this phenomenology. Not only does it seek to "put essences back into existence," (PP, vii), to think back to the lifeworld, but the weighting of genesis ultimately overcomes the sense of attained essence entirely. That "the greatest lesson which reduction teaches us is the impossibility of a complete reduction" (PP, xiv) is not so much a negative comment upon Husserl as it is the affirmation of what Merleau-Ponty understands an *existential* phenomenology to be.

This use of a phenomenologically described genesis *is* both what uncovers and justifies the sense of embodied meaning Merleau-Ponty elaborates. Symptomatically it is instructive to note the main class of examples which he uses to illustrate the phenomenon of expressive embodiment. The paradigms come from learning new meanings: (1) the child learning speech, (2) on first understanding others, (3) learning a new language, (4) learning a new philosophy, (5) the lover revealing his feelings, (6) the writer or philosopher struggling with awakening a sense of primordial experience, and finally (7) the mythical "first man who spoke." (PP, 178-9) These examples, adumbrated in varying ways, once again are illustrations of the stylistic movement of Merleau-Ponty's thought: the movement from an initial ambiguity through struggle towards a birth of new meaning. Thus for a third time we are re-plunged into the thematic problem of speaking in such a way that the new may be expressed. How does one give birth to the position which is phenomenology?

C. *Thought in speech*

If a theory of embodied meaning is central—"the word has a meaning"—there remains a need to outline the configuration of that embodiment. Merleau-Ponty notes "there is thus, either in the man who listens or reads, or in the one who speaks or writes, a *thought in speech* the existence of which is unsuspected by intellectualism." (PP, 179) Thought-in-speech to coin a language version of being in the world, is the expressive dimension of human existence. What is embodied expression?

1. First, it is clearly a behavior or performance of the living subject. Language in Merleau-Ponty's sense, is not something *had* by a subject; it is the subject in action. Speech in the broad sense used by Merleau-Ponty is the *performance* of thought. "Thus speech, in the speaker does not

translate ready-made thought, but accomplishes it." (PP, 178) The same performative emphasis is found in the interpretation of naming, that speech-act so often taken as central to linguistically oriented philosophies. "The denomination of objects does not follow upon recognition; it is itself recognition." (PP, 177) "For the child a thing is not known until it is named, the name is the essence of the thing and resides in it on the same footing as its colour and its form. For pre-scientific thinking, naming an object is causing it to exist or changing it." (PP, 178) Naming *is* a performance.

2. The expressive activity of the subject in speech is intentional, directed and focused activity. And as with all phenomenological intentionality, such an action is both "internal" and "external," or better, already outside the enclosed self-directed toward the world. The performance of thought "internally" is as linguistic as actually spoken thought. "Thought is not 'internal' then, and does not exist independently of the world and of words . . . we can silently recall to ourselves . . . through which we acquire the illusion of an inner life. But in reality this supposed silence is alive with words, this inner life is an inner language." (PP, 183) "Inner speech" is also embodied expression. Language is not private—nor is it public—it is between subjects, intersubjective, it is "a synchronizing of my own existence, a transformation of my being. We live in a world where speech is an institution." (PP, 183-4)[6]

3. One can better say, rather than that man has or uses language, that man *is* language. "Language is much more like a sort of being than a means. . ." (S, 43) The thought-in-speech is a style of living in language. "The linguistic and inter-subjective world no longer surprises us, we no longer distinguish it from the world itself, and it is within a world already spoken and speaking what we think." (PP, 184) This thought-in-speech in which we live is itself quite concrete and even particular. "We may speak several languages, but one of them always remains the one in which we live. In order completely to assimilate a language, it would be necessary to make the world it expresses one's own." (PP, 187) Embodied expression is concrete and positional, the place from which one "views" the world. There is no metalanguage of disembodied meanings

---

6. Although "institution" draws some of its meaning from its common meaning, Merleau-Ponty apparently uses it to express a nuanced "realism" in contrast to Husserl's supposed "idealism." In *The Visible and the Invisible* the sense of meaning instituted within the human world balances the husserlian "constitution" of the subject.

floating over and apart from actual languages. "If there is such a thing as universal thought, it is achieved by taking up the effort towards expression and communication in one single language, and accepting all its ambiguities, all the suggestions and overtones of meaning of which a linguistic tradition is made up, and which are the exact measure of its power of expression." (PP, 188) Thought-in-speech is embodied language. Thought *is* body in the same way that the subject *is* body.

If linguistic dualism is rejected—there is no realm of ideal and complete meanings above and apart from actual language, nor is there a realm of pure physical non-meaningful motion which may be "used" by mentally employed meanings. And if all language in the human sense is existentially embodied, then the result is that the performances, positionings, and utterings we make are all made "inside" this existential language. Our being is being-*in*-the-world, here our thought is *in* language. But this poses an enigma: "One would have to know the language in order to learn it." (S, 39)

Merleau-Ponty accepts this enigma. "This sort of circle, according to which language, in the presence of those who are learning it, precedes itself, teaches itself, and suggests its own deciphering, is perhaps the marvel which defines language." (S, 39) Language does convey itself. Although there are several neat conceptual devices developed by Merleau-Ponty to justify this totality of engagement within language—for example, the first word of a child functions as a sentence, the part is already a whole (S, 40)—it is more important to grasp the internal movement which characterizes the birth of speech.

This movement, again the birth of meaning, is one which follows the pattern *from ambiguity towards clarity*. In Merleau-Ponty's phraseology this is the movement *from silence to speech*. Several important aspects of this movement need note:

4. Strictly speaking there is no state prior to being found within existential language. We have been led astray by those who have spoken of a "pre-linguistic" state insofar as we have been led to believe that this state is equivalent to a state prior to meaning.[7] There is, in Merleau-Ponty, the movement from silence to speech, but that is not a movement from non-meaning to meaning, it is rather a movement from the implicit

---

7. I have been guilty of this error on several occasions as well. ("Language and Experience" in *New Essays in Phenomenology*, Quadrangle, 1970). A pre-linguistic level would be the equivalent within phenomenology of the empiricist sense datum.

to the explicit, from ambiguity already *pregnant* with significance to the expressed significance of speech. If meaning is "born" it is because the world is already "pregnant" with that possibility.

Meaning, in an existential theory of language, is the entire movement from silence to speech. It is a ratio of the implicit to the explicit. Thought in the usual sense, is but a focus within the totality of meaning. "Because meaning is the total movement of speech, our thought crawls along in language. Yet for the same reason, our thought moves through language as a gesture goes beyond the individual point of its passage." (S, 43)

5. It is within the context of this movement from implicit to explicit significance that the continuum of metaphors and behaviors which surround explicit speech take shape. "Gesture," "gestural meaning," even the "indirect voices of silence" in painting, and the concrete meanings of music which so well illustrate the incarnation of sound and meaning are all in between silence and speech. They are meaning-activities of the subject, but short of the explicitness of speech.

6. If the first movement is from implicit to explicit, from silence to speech, a reverse side of that movement remains implied in every speech-act. There is no final, no complete expression. "Now if we rid our minds of the idea that our language is the translation or cipher of an original text, we shall see that the idea of complete expression is nonsensical. . ." (S, 43) The existentiality of language is such that the field of implicit silence is always broader than the focus of explicit speech. In this sense speech is essentially finite even if also open and indeterminate.

7. It also means that the broad field of silent implicit meaning lies as present background to all that is actually said. "Behind" what is said lies the unsaid. For Merleau-Ponty this is to imply that all speech, all explicit language, is *indirect*. "But what if language expresses as much by what is between words as by words themselves? By that which it does not 'say' as by what it 'says'? . . . All language is indirect or allusive—that is, if you wish, silence." (S, 45, 43)

The existentiality of Merleau-Ponty's language theory begins in "anti-cartesianism." In this it is part of the entire movement of phenomenology to counter the dualistic division of man and his world into matter and mind and instead to reassert the essential insertion of man within his world as incarnate being in a lifeworld. The existentiality of Merleau-Ponty's language theory ends in the affirmation of embodied expression, thought-in-speech and speech-in-silence, which attempts for language what is also attempted for the subject in the world.

PHENOMENOLOGY AND EXISTENTIAL LANGUAGE

All the various parts and aspects of Merleau-Ponty's theory of language may be seen as a gestalt, a coherent whole, when viewed as the exemplification of a basic phenomenological model. For the sake of simplicity I shall use the terms, field and focus. The field is the totality of presence which may be differentiated according to the question addressed to this totality of presence. Thus, if our question is visual, the field is the whole of the visual field before one. Focus is the region within the field which is attended to. Again, if the example is visual, the focal center may be a certain object which stands out against the background of the visual field. (I have characterized both here in noematic terms, but the noetic reflexiveness might also be characterized. For example, that which stands out must be correlated to my act of attending.) Extended, the notion, field, is the phenomenological "world," focus, the phenomenologically explicit attention within the world.

"Silence," in Merleau-Ponty's use, is the field of pregnant, latent expressiveness always already present to the living subject. Pregnant silence is always and wholly present—man lives within the world of implicitly meaningful silence. "In short, we must consider speech before it is spoken, the background of silence which does not cease to surround it and without which it would say nothing." (S, 46) "Speech" is the focal center, the explicit foreground of meaning which floats, varies, is directed but which always stands out against the background of silence. The clarity of explicit meaning is a relative clarity, relative to the implicitness of the background. "The clearness of language stands out from an obscure background, and if we carry our research far enough we shall eventually find that language is equally uncommunicative of anything other than itself, that its meaning is inseparable from it." (PP, 188) The movement of speech is a movement from and upon the field of silence.

This is also the reason why speech is taking a position. Focusing is taking a position within the field, it is a selection. But it, too, is relative. The position does not remove or obliterate the field, it merely allows it to remain background. The "indirection" of silence behind speech is not removable and equally the explicitness of focus is not capable of completeness. If speech is necessarily focus it can easily be seen that completeness of expression is impossible. "Completeness" belongs latently only to silence, to the unsaid.

The focus against the field may be exceedingly fine or broadened. Thus within speech itself—better speech within language—the focus is the moving ray situated within the world of silent meaning. "Since the sign has meaning only insofar as it is profiled against other signs, its meaning is entirely involved in language. Speech always comes into play against a background of speech; it is always only a fold in the immense fabric of language." (S, 42)

From the primordial field of silence to the most explicit attainment of thought-in-speech also lies a concentric and leveled set of stratifications. Gestural meaning, if "lower" than speech, is also broader. Within speech itself such stratifications also occur: "any linguistic operation presupposes the apprehension of a significance, but that significance in both cases is, as it were, specialized: there are different layers of significance, from the visual to the conceptual by way of verbal concept." (PP, 195) But these stratifications are merely finessed distinctions within the broader concept of field and focus which are called for to differentiate the degree and range of the focal center.

All expressivity, whether "higher" or "lower," more or less finely focused, is a positioning within the world of pregnant silence. Concretely, in man's case, thought-word-sound in existential speech is the region where expressivity is most clearly heard. The posturing which is speech *is* singing the world and "singing the world" is now stronger than metaphor.

One may even speak here of expressivity as an "essence" of man in spite of Merleau-Ponty's demure concerning essences. Expressivity is at the least a dimension of being-in-the-world which takes distinctive human shape in speech. But it may be more than *a* dimension.

LANGUAGE AND PERCEPTION

In Merleau-Ponty's corpus of writing the question of language was imbedded in and followed from his discoveries within the perceptual world. Expressivity in *Phenomenology of Perception* was but one chapter, even that titled "the *body* as expression, and speech (emphasis mine)." The other explicit essays, paragraphs, comments also constitute but a small amount of the whole. Yet there is reason to believe that the reversed role of language in relation to perception taken here shows something at work in Merleau-Ponty's thought as well.

If expression is always embodied and if the world itself is that field of pregnant silence, then language in its broadened sense is not just one dimension of being.[8] My claim is that the result of taking language in the way Merleau-Ponty has *is to have made the question of perception enigmatic.* Furthermore, I believe that Merleau-Ponty in the later works had himself begun to re-evaluate the role of perception, Perception, in *The Visible and the Invisible,* becomes the "perceptual faith." But faith recognized as faith is already doubt. 'Philosophy is the perceptual faith questioning itself about itself. One can say of it, as of every faith, that it is a faith *because* it is the possibility of doubt. . ." (VI, 103)

The doubt is such that perception and language are tied together more intimately, more inextricably than ever. If perception is "primary" it is not bare perception. Although Merleau-Ponty maintains his notion of inquiring back and down into the levels of experience—to the degree that he leaves himself open to those who see him seeking a level of pre-meaning—that which is found is found always sayable. Philosophy "asks of our experience of the world that the world is before it is a thing one speaks of and which is taken for granted, before it has been reduced to a set of manageable, disposable significations; it directs this question to our mute life, it addresses itself to that compound of the world and of ourselves that precedes reflection. . ." (VI, 102) But what it finds there is already open to speech. "But in addition, what it finds in thus returning to the sources, *it says* [emphasis mine]." (VI, 102)

What is at issue can be put quite simply if viewed tangentially in terms of another broadly accepted philosophical distinction. Phenomenology in its "anti-cartesianism" claims to have re-discovered the living subject in a lifeworld. This re-discovery claims the power to overthrow the "cartesian" notions of psycho-physical dualism, "mind" and "matter" are to be transcended. However, a similar and no less tenacious distinction haunts our intellectual world as well; the distinction between *nature* and *culture.* Broader in its way, and thus perhaps more difficult to dispel, this dichotemy must fall, too, if phenomenology is to work out

---

8. Perception-language specifically melt together in "silence." The working notes to *The Visible and Invisible* equate "brute," "wild" Being with the perceived world (VI, 171). "Silence" is thus the primordial field for *both* perception and speech.

its program. Given this distinction, perception in its way belongs roughly to nature, while language belongs more clearly to culture.[9] Thus language is "added" to nature.

There is evidence, in Merleau-Ponty, of ambivalence in relation to the tradition of nature-culture. In his essay, "The Primacy of Perception" he appears to overtly appeal to the distinction (EP, 42, 49); in *Phenomenology and Perception* he speaks of speech as "the surplus of our existence over natural being" (PP, 197) and links language to "a linguistic and cultural world" (PP, 197); but increasingly the implication is one which must eventually call the nature-culture dualism into question. From the beginning he admits that human perception is different from animal perception—though without linking this to culture as such. But in *The Visible and the Invisible* perception becomes enigmatic precisely in relation to "cultural" factors. For example, in noting dramatic changes in the history of art regarding perspective. "I say that the Renaissance perspective is a cultural fact, that perception is polymorphic and that if it becomes Euclidian, this is because it allows itself to be oriented by the system." (VI, 212) Perception here is strongly relative to "culture." But inversely, Merleau-Ponty notes, "What I maintain is that: there is an informing of perception by culture which enables us to say *that culture is perceived*" [emphasis mine]. (VI, 212)

Nowhere, to my knowledge, does Merleau-Ponty make a sustained attack upon nature-culture as upon the previous distinction of psychophysical dualism—but the ambiguity of perception, now tied more thoroughly to that of meaning-language—"culture" calls for that attack to be made. But how? The answer is found in the guiding theme of the need for a radical language in phenomenology. If we are to "see" in a new way we must be able to "say" in a new way. A language needs to be born.

Man as language has this capacity. His perceptual-meanings (the *lifeworld* in the best husserlian sense) are open to the creation of the new. Merleau-Ponty was on this track when he was untimely taken:

> If this paradox is not an impossibility, and if philosophy can speak, it is because language is not only the depository of fixed and acquired significations, because its cumulative power itself results

---

9. In actuality this assignment of areas is not as clear as it first seems. As we discover more about animal "languages" and behavior on one hand and more about man's primitivism on the other, the distinction is open even to empirical question.

from a power of anticipation or of pre-possession, because one speaks not only of what one knows, so as to set out a display of it—but also of what one does not know, in order to know it—and because language in forming itself expresses, at least laterally, an ontogenesis of which it is a part. (VI, 102)

Phenomenology as philosophical revolution in its "linguistic tactics" is implicitly and purposefully radical in direction. It is precisely the taken for granted which must be uprooted and, if need be, overthrown. "Cartesian" clarity is sometimes polarly opposite the *poesis* necessary to radicality. "But from this it follows that the words most charged with philosophy are not necessarily those that contain what they say, but rather those that most energetically open upon Being, because they more closely convey the life of the whole and make our habitual evidences vibrate until they disjoin." (VI, 102)

What Merleau-Ponty begins to seek explicitly lay earlier in latent form in both the phenomenological turn and in the question of embodied, expressive being. What must be said may be said, but not in terms of what merely has been said. What is called for, given the "logic" of Merleau-Ponty's thought is "wild meaning."

> In a sense the whole of philosophy, as Husserl says, consists in restoring a power to signify a birth of meaning, or a wild meaning, an expression of experience by experience, which in particular clarifies the special domain of language. And it is as Valery said, language is everything, since it is the very voice of the things, the waves, and the forests. And what we have to understand is that there is no dialectical reversal from one of these views to the other; we do not have to reassemble them into a synthesis: they are two aspects of the reversibility which is the ultimate truth. (VI, 155)

Key to Text Quotations

The direct quotations from Merleau-Ponty have been noted in the text. Abbreviations are as follows:

EP   Maurice Merleau-Ponty, "The Primacy of Perception," trans. James M. Edie, *Existential Phenomenology* (London: Prentice-Hall, 1967).

PP ———. *The Phenomenology of Perception*, Trans. Colin Smith (London: Routledge and Kegen Paul, 1962).
S ———, *Signs*, trans, Richard C. McCleary (Evanston: Northwestern University Press, 1964).
VI ———, *The Visible and the Invisible*, trans. Alphonso Lingis (Evanston: Northwestern University Press, 1968).

About the Author

Don Ihde is professor of philosophy at the State University of New York at Stony Brook. His articles have appeared in a wide variety of journals and in numerous anthologies of phenomenolical essays. He is the author of *Hermeneutic Phenomenology* published by Northwestern University Press and the co-editor of *Phenomenology and Existentialism* published by Capricorn Books. He has been the holder of a Fulbright Research Fellowship in France and was a Senior Fellow of the National Endowment for the Humanities in England. His most recent work has been upon human-machine relations and the experience of technology.

Index

A

Abraham 46
Abschattungen 59
Adam 108
akoumena 26
Anschauung 25
Aristotle 24-26, 36, 43, 128
auditory imagination 25, 32-34, 36, 38-40, 47, 52-55, 57, 80
Austin, John 35, 135, 142, 159-160

B

Beethoven, Ludwig 27-28
Békésy, Georg 73
Berkeley, George 24, 146
Bible 42
brackets, bracketing 27, 84, 95, 145, 150

C

Camus, Albert 118
Carnap, Rudolph 131
core-fringe structure 49, 96
corps vécu 126, 166

D

demythologization 109-110
Descartes, Rene 118-120, 128

descriptive psychology 13, 15-16
descriptive rule 16-17
Dewey, John 13
Dufrenne, Michel 133

E

echo-phenomenon 76, 79
eidetic intuition 94
Eidos 25
Empedocles 25
empiricism 125, 147-148, 168
epoché 62-63, 94, 120
essence, 14
  inexact 18, 148
existentialism 25, 117

F

Faust 108
field-state 99, 104
free fantasy 14

G

gestalt function 116
Greeks 13, 43, 65

H

Hamann, J. G. 133
Heaton, J. M. 92

Hebrews 31, 43
Heidegger, Martin 70, 83, 87, 117-120, 123-124, 127-130, 133, 146, 158, 164, 166
Heraclitus 24, 26
Husserl, Edmund 16, 25, 30, 33-34, 59, 70, 77, 93, 118-124, 126, 133, 138, 142-146, 149, 153-154, 157, 161, 164, 166, 170, 178

I

inner speech 32-33, 38-40, 55-59, 80
intentionality 70, 96, 122, 150, 153, 156
invariants 18, 24, 100
Isaac 46
Isaiah 44

J

Jacob 46
James, William 13
Job 46
Joyce, James 57

K

Kant, Immanuel 118, 119, 128
Kierkegaard, Soren 50
Künste 34

L

Lichtung 42
logical atomism 131, 133, 136
Logos 31, 109, 125
lumen naturale 43

M

Marx, Karl 102
Mead, George H. 13
Merleau-Ponty, Maurice 34, 37, 42, 51, 74, 77, 83, 117-118, 120, 123-127, 130, 152, 158, 163-170, 172, 175-178
Moses 42

N

New Testament 43
Neurath, Otto 141
noema 50, 120
noematic-noetic correlation 138

O

Ong, Walter 40
Old Testament 31, 46

P

Parmenides 69-71, 73, 75-76, 80-83, 85-90
Peirce, Charles S. 25
Pfänder, Alexander 142
phenomenological reduction 15, 26-27, 63, 94, 120, 144, 157, 170
phenomenological psychology 23
Plato 33, 113
Prometheus 108

Q

Quine, Willard van Orman 131-132, 135-141

R

Rede 127
Ricoeur, Paul 35, 102, 108-112, 116, 118, 130-131, 133, 138-142, 158, 161
Ruf 127
Russell, Bertrand 131, 145
Ryle, Gilbert 35

S

Sartre, Jean-Paul 25, 37, 40, 118
Sicht 25, 59
Simplicius 82
Smith, F. Joseph 26, 29, 31
Spiegelberg, Herbert 142-143
Spinoza, Benedict 115
Strawson, P. F. 35
Streisand, Barbara 102

T

Theophrastus 82

V

variations,
  fantasy 53
  free 52, 54, 71, 147, 150
  imaginative 17, 33
  perspective 14, 17, 64, 94

Vivaldi 78
vouloir-dire 158

W

Wesenschau 25, 59, 71
Wisdom, John 35
Wittgenstein, Ludwig 131, 134-135, 142-154, 159

LIBRARY OF DAVIDSON COLLEGE

Books on regular loan may be checked out for **two weeks**. Books must be presented at the Circulation Desk in order to be renewed.

A fine is charged after date due.

Special books are subject to special regulations at the discretion of library staff.